I plead with Euodia and I plead with Syntyche to be of the same mind in the Lord. Yes, and I ask you, my true companion, help these women since they have contended at my side in the cause of the gospel, along with Clement and the rest of my co-workers, whose names are in the book of life.

—Philippians 4:2–3 (NIV)

Extraordinary Women OF THE BIBLE

HIGHLY FAVORED: MARY'S STORY

SINS AS SCARLET: RAHAB'S STORY

A HARVEST OF GRACE: RUTH AND NAOMI'S STORY

AT HIS FEET: MARY MAGDALENE'S STORY

TENDER MERCIES: ELIZABETH'S STORY

WOMAN OF REDEMPTION: BATHSHEBA'S STORY

JEWEL OF PERSIA: ESTHER'S STORY

A HEART RESTORED: MICHAL'S STORY

BEAUTY'S SURRENDER: SARAH'S STORY

THE WOMAN WARRIOR: DEBORAH'S STORY

THE GOD WHO SEES: HAGAR'S STORY

THE FIRST DAUGHTER: EVE'S STORY

THE ONES JESUS LOVED: MARY AND MARTHA'S STORY

THE BEGINNING OF WISDOM: BILQIS'S STORY

THE SHADOW'S SONG: MAHLAH AND NO'AH'S STORY

DAYS OF AWE: EUODIA AND SYNTYCHE'S STORY

Extraordinary Women OF THE BIBLE

DAYS OF AWE

EUODIA AND SYNTYCHE'S STORY

Texie Susan Gregory

Guideposts

Published by Guideposts
100 Reserve Road, Suite E200
Danbury, CT 06810
Guideposts.org

Cover and interior design by Müllerhaus
Cover illustration by Brian Call represented by Illustration Online LLC.
Typeset by Aptara, Inc.

ISBN 978-1-961126-42-8 (hardcover)
ISBN 978-1-961126-43-5 (epub)

Printed and bound in the United States of America
10 9 8 7 6 5 4 3 2

Extraordinary Women OF THE BIBLE

DAYS OF AWE

EUODIA AND SYNTYCHE'S STORY

DEDICATION

To my cherished daughter, Texie Elizabeth Soltis,
and
To my sisters
The steps
The in-laws
The half
The spiritual
The heart-knit
The writers
Those who help me laugh
The few in whom I confide
The many in ministry
The military ones
The new ones
The lifelong ones

ACKNOWLEDGMENTS

A million? A billion? Not even a trillion words would begin to express my gratitude for those who come alongside me as I write. You are faithful. You are prayer warriors. You are a joy to know and work alongside. You are the friends of my heart and friends I've never met.

Beloved prayer team: Stacie Ciesynski, Sheri Shannon, Linda Vanderhoof, and Kay White.

Treasured beta readers: Donna Holland, Texie Soltis, and Victoria Warren.

Delightful and dedicated editorial team at Guideposts: Jane Haertel, Sabrina Diaz, and Ellen Tarver.

Deeply appreciated agent: Bob Hostetler with the Steve Laube Agency.

Cast of CHARACTERS

Clement • church leader and teacher tasked to help Euodia and Syntyche

Euodia • one of two women named in Philippians 4:2

Syntyche • one of two women named in Philippians 4:2

Syzygus • means "yokefellow," leader asked to help Euodia and Syntyche

Biblical References

Epaphroditus • fellow worker with Paul and messenger to Philippi

Lydia • seller of purple, first Christian convert in Europe, baptized in Philippi

Paul • apostle, missionary to both Jews and Gentiles

Silas • Christian leader who accompanied Paul on second missionary journey

Timothy • Christian leader who accompanied Paul on second missionary journey

Major Characters

Cerberus • persecutor of Christ followers

Claudia • servant in Euodia's house

Helena • Clement's mother

Malitta • friend of Syntyche

Marcellus • Euodia's husband

Tymon • Euodia and Syntyche's older brother

Valeria • friend of Euodia

Minor Characters

Albus • owner of bath

Alex • Syntyche's late husband

Amelia • Marcellus's mother

Atticus • Marcellus's father

Demi • servant in Tymon's house

Linus • Euodia's dog

Mania • relative of Albus

Marcus • friend of Tymon

Glossary of TERMS

carpentum • richly adorned, covered carriage used by Roman matrons

cisium • light, open carriage for two people

kunun • a vicious dog

mal aria • bad air (malaria)

mekici • flat doughy cake filled with yogurt

Matronalia • festival for Juno on March 1st

palla • a long-sleeved mantle

patrician • an aristocrat or noble

stola • long pleated robe worn over a tunic by married women

thermopolium • a counter where hot ready-to-eat food is served

vardar • cold, northwesterly wind that blows from mountains to valleys of Macedonia

CHAPTER ONE

April AD 60

Deep, guttural sobs grated the room's air. Euodia knelt by the burly man's pallet and placed a hand on his sweat-drenched forehead to soothe him.

"Hush, Rafe. All is well. You're safe. Safe and healing."

"Not Rafe. Cerberus." His voice bore the hoarseness of disuse.

She sat back on her heels and frowned, uncertain—no, hoping—she'd misunderstood. "Cerberus, the *kunun*?"

He grunted once. Cerberus. The unofficial hound of Christ followers who, like his name, was a hunter, tracking down believers to harass and oppress. The man who ten years ago dragged Paul before the magistrates after he freed a slave from an evil spirit.

Cerberus opened one swollen eye and glared at her. She averted her gaze but refused to surrender to instinct and skitter backward. If he suspected she was a Christ follower, he'd shun her help and drag himself back to the alley where Brother Clement found him bleeding from knife wounds.

The flat-footed slap of bare feet alerted Euodia to her sister's approach. She stood abruptly, placing herself between the entrance and Cerberus's face to block his view. He must not see Syntyche. Her fearless, determined sister would so offend him by proclaiming Jesus as God that she'd be arrested for being a nuisance.

"Dear one." She'd not use her sister's name and further endanger her. "Please, come with me into the courtyard. I must tell you who..."

Syntyche brushed past her. "You are Cerberus. I am Syntyche." She paused. "A Christ follower."

Euodia's shoulders slumped.

His battered face tightened, curling the split lip into a bloody snarl. Euodia tugged at her sister's arm. Syntyche jerked free.

"Leave us." She motioned toward the door. "Brother Clement is waiting outside."

Euodia reached the door before realizing she'd once again obeyed her sister without question. She turned back, hesitant to leave her sister alone with Cerberus. He was a threat, even badly beaten and wounded.

Syntyche knew her well. She'd turned as if waiting to shoo her out the door. A flick of Syntyche's wrist and Euodia scurried away. Lingering would earn her a sharp reproof.

Clement stood when she entered the atrium.

Questions rose and toppled, jumbling for first utterance until all she managed was, "I don't understand."

He nodded. "Brother Syzygus is a man I respect. Together we chose to withhold the patient's name, thinking you'd be more comfortable not knowing who he was. Two weeks is a long time to be anxious in someone's presence, even if he was unconscious much of that time."

"So, you knew his name from the beginning, and you told my sister. You trusted her with his name but not me."

"I did. Forgive me, please." Despite his words, he did not appear contrite. "It was to ease your way, but it was wrong. You said he'd be here another week. Someone can guard you while you tend to him."

Euodia folded her arms across her chest, unwilling to be placated. "And you brought him into your home, and he knows our names."

"Not yours."

"You have put us all at risk with your decision. Even your *mater.*"

Clement ran a hand over his lightly graying beard. "Sister Euodia, I have learned the hard way to do nothing without seeking the Lord's guidance first. I was led down an alley I never walk and found a man I never wanted to meet—much less help. This is not my doing. Look for the Lord's hand in this, and wait with great expectation for what He will do."

Euodia crossed the room to a padded bench and sank into its softness. Leaning her head against the frescoed wall, she counted and recounted the red, yellow, and blue circles ornamenting the ceiling. After a few minutes, she lifted her head and pinned him with her gaze.

"My sister is alone with our greatest oppressor. What do you think she can do?"

Clement raised an eyebrow. "Is there anything your sister can't do when the Lord guides her?"

His words stung. Even the church leaders believed Syntyche to be always capable, always confident, always perfect.

Syntyche studied the man before her, then bowed her head asking for guidance. Looking at him again, she saw beneath the battered face covered with stubbled beard, past the Roman-styled hair, beyond the tense lips, to a child—an angry, confused little boy.

"Cerberus, I'm going to tell you a story. You can listen or sleep or interrupt, but I will not stop speaking."

He neither acquiesced nor objected. She'd not expected a response.

"You and I may live as Romans, but we are Greek—from name to nose. We know the stories of our ancestors and the gods of our people. Like you, I have offered incense and votives at the temples, sung hymns, and celebrated the festivals." She leaned closer. "This is what I learned. We must go to our gods and do and give and beg and bribe them for favor and grovel to avoid their wrath. It is the way of life, yes?"

Cerberus gave an infinitesimal nod.

"There is another way, a God who came to love us—Jesus, the Savior."

His cheeks drew inward, his jaw worked and spit hurled forth. Syntyche wiped it from her face. It was not the first time she'd been spat upon. Her people believed spitting thwarted an evil presence.

"As Greeks, we worship many gods. Our loyalty is divided, and we cannot keep each one content. Grace does not exist. With the Christ, there is no guilt, no wrath, no condemnation. Let me tell you how this came to be and how it has changed my life.

"Darkness covered the souls of all people. Fathomless darkness so deep no light could penetrate. Yet something dwelled within each person, an inexplicable desire they could grasp only a sliver of—a yearning for light."

She knew he heard the story she told. At times his hands twitched or his body shifted. His shoulders would tense, and then his very stillness assured her he listened.

She finished and withdrew without a farewell. Lingering in the atrium, she walked beside the pool of water, needing a moment alone before joining Clement, his mater, Helena, and Euodia in the gardens where they'd been praying for her witness. Tomorrow and every day Cerberus remained under Clement's roof, she'd share a bit more—her story, Saul's transformation to Paul, Jesus's harder teachings.

Syntyche traced a blue swirl on one of the columns. She'd always been bold, making a choice and advancing undeterred. Faith was harder, waiting to be shown His way, allowing only His words to pass her lips. It frightened her—this vulnerability—this walking blindly with the Lord and only Him. Since her husband's death five years ago…

"Syntyche!"

She blushed when Clement spoke her name and again upon realizing Euodia's eyes lit with mischief. If her little sister said anything to Clement or Helena, she'd…

Euodia crossed the room and touched her elbow. "Did he hear you, Sister?"

"How could he not? I'm not known for being soft-spoken." She laughed then sobered. "The question is, did he hear the Lord?"

Euodia pulled back. "Of course that's what I meant." She glanced up at the light flowing through the roof opening. "Forgive me, but I need to return home. My husband will wonder where I am. You will return tomorrow?"

"As long as I have a captive audience, he will hear my witness. If he turns away from the Lord, it will not be from ignorance. Euodia, how much longer before he is well enough to be moved?"

Clement answered for her. "His family returned from their travels early. They sent word they are hiring physicians and preparing a room for him. Mater spoke with them and insisted he was not ready to travel, but his wife was adamant he'd be better off with them. A covered litter will arrive for him in three days."

Syntyche grinned. "Three days? An auspicious number for Cerberus to be spiritually dead and then receive eternal life, Lord willing."

The next day, Euodia rubbed her sweaty palms against her clothes and tried to still the fluttering in her stomach before opening the door to Cerberus's cubicle. Knowing who he was bothered her more than she wanted to admit. It was not the giving of her time and skills that concerned her, it was fear of reprisal—of the humiliation of being whipped and the subsequent pain that lingered for weeks. She'd tended believers who'd been flogged and seen the agony as she mended their torn flesh. Cerberus was known throughout Philippi as a cunning hunter whose prey suffered when they were caught.

Legs trembling, she forced herself to approach his pallet and kneel beside him as she'd done each day for over two weeks. She swallowed, pulled at the neck of her clothes. Was the room always so warm?

This time, there was no grunt of acknowledgment or raised hand to greet her. She loosened the bandages to reapply honey on the wounds she'd stitched. He did not flinch. She probed the swelling in his arm. He said nothing. He did not blink when she soothed salve over the cuts on his face.

"Are you in pain?" She examined the gashes, but no red streaks of infection radiated from the wounds. "Are you thirsty? Hungry? Chilled?"

No answer. Perhaps he was embarrassed a woman tended him. Or, maybe he was miffed she'd referred to him as a kunun, a vicious dog. She'd assumed he'd be proud of the epithet since his was the name of the multiheaded dog who guarded Hades to prevent the dead from escape.

Her work complete, she gathered pouches of herbs and ointment jars and returned them to her medical box. Silently, she studied him.

Yesterday, had her sister so offended him with her witness that he refused to speak? She shrugged. Syntyche would return to share the story of their Lord. If Cerberus was annoyed about hearing it once, he'd soon be livid.

"Syntyche will return today."

The pulse in his neck quickened.

"She will not be deterred. Our Lord means everything to her—to us—and she will tell you about Him no matter what you do to her later. She knows the danger she faces by speaking of Him—especially to you."

He said not a word. It was as if she did not exist, had not spoken, had not been heard.

Syntyche shivered in the morning chill. Again today, she'd speak of salvation and the Anointed One, the Savior, to Euodia's patient. Yesterday, Cerberus's barely suppressed rage had not frightened her. Fury meant something touched an ache deep inside him.

She'd been angry when told she needed a savior. How dare anyone suggest she could not please the gods on her own strength? No one tried harder than she to excel, until, disheartened and disenchanted, she no longer desired to please anyone or anything. The Christ was different, offering salvation and hope when tragedy splintered her life.

Helena's handmaid opened the door when Syntyche reached Clement's house. The scent of quince—apples and oranges and vanilla—wafted through the house. These gently warming months with their earthy fragrance were her favorite time of year.

She slipped off her sandals and paused a moment by the smoldering brazier to pray.

Lord, guide my every word.

Cerberus lay propped against a pile of pillows. Seeing her, he immediately turned his head to the wall and closed his eyes. As the swelling in his face had lessened, she could see his jaw tighten.

If he thought ignoring her would offend or stop her from speaking, he would soon realize his mistake. Nothing stopped God's gift from being shared.

She sat an arm's length from his side and began.

"Darkness covered the souls of all people. Fathomless darkness..." She repeated each word of the story, and even though he did not watch her, she knew the joy and sorrow of the story showed on her face and burst through her voice.

"Then the Creator of all—the Creator of mercy and grace—heard the cries of desperation." She choked, remembering her own darkness and desperation. "He became an infant, a helpless one, like we were helpless."

She felt Him speaking through her, her own voice familiar to her but the words not her own. She was a channel, an aqueduct of His message to this man.

The story complete, she rose and left the room without another word.

Staring into the atrium's pool, she wondered if the seeds of Christ had taken root. In a moment of fear, she wrapped her arms around herself. Would Cerberus be saved, or she killed?

Rose perfume reached her before Helena called a greeting. “Syntyche, come and break your fast with me. I have food laid out for us in the alcove.”

The two women gathered around a meal of cheese, grapes, freshly squeezed juice, and *mekici.* The flat, doughy cakes, fried until they were a light gold, oozed with creamy yogurt. Syntyche licked her lips, savoring the treat.

“The best part, Helena, is that someone else made them.”

“If you weren’t known to be such a good cook, others wouldn’t be afraid to prepare food for you. I dared not tell my cook that Syntyche would be eating these. She’d have gone to bed insisting her head throbbed, and we’d have not seen her until you left.”

Syntyche reached across the table and caught Helena’s blue-veined hand between her. “Tell me the truth. Am I that frightening?”

“Yes, dear, you are.” Helena squeezed the younger woman’s hands. “No, now do not pull away. Listen to me. You are fearless in speaking of our Lord. That shames those of us who are not as bold—especially the men. You are the most excellent cook in Philippi—better than anyone twice your age.” She cocked her head. “How *do* you know exactly which seasonings are best and what amount to use? You are young enough to remarry. That unnerves the younger women.”

“I do not mean to—”

“These are all good things. Our Lord has given you many gifts to use for Him. Do not hesitate or fear to do so.”

“Sometimes I fear, Helena.” She whispered as if afraid to hear her own words. “I fear speaking out for our Lord will lead to my death and there will not be time to say goodbye to those I love."

Helena reached over and lifted Syntyche's chin. "Then you must love them well each day."

"Today is our farewell." Euodia massaged the lightly scabbed wounds framing Cerberus's face. "The swelling is down, and your color is better. Keep honey on the gashes I stitched."

"Traitor."

His growled insult was loud. Good—he gathered strength.

She held her breath against his stench and moved closer to clean the last trace of pus from a slash beneath his arm. He'd refused her attempts to bathe him since regaining consciousness.

Euodia chuckled to herself. When he was well enough to return to the baths, all the water would need to be replaced, soiled from his weeks-long sweat.

"I'm not a traitor. I'm a loyal citizen." She held up a hand. "Save your breath. I'm not an atheist either, as you've repeatedly accused me. I worship a different God than you."

"You believe what your sister says?"

"Not a word of it." Enjoying the shock in his eyes, she waited a moment before continuing. "Not because she said it. I believe what the Lord has revealed to me, what I've heard read from the Hebrew scriptures, and what Paul taught us of the Anointed One."

"Paul." He snorted.

"Tomorrow you return to your family." She bit her tongue, refusing to beg for leniency when eventually he'd order her and her sister to be arrested. Her sister might brave the prisons, but Syntyche never feared anything. Not trusting herself to do more than nod farewell, she stood, gathered her healing supplies and left the room.

After blowing a kiss to Helena, she stepped outside and inhaled the air's freshness. If she hurried, she'd be home before her husband knew how long she'd been away. He knew she was a Christ follower but not how much time she spent among the believers. Shaking off a twinge of guilt, she walked faster. Besides, Marcellus had spent the morning attending an interview, and she wanted to know how he felt about it.

Syntyche brushed the street dust from her clothes and watched Euodia scurry away. As much time as her sister had invested in the patient, had she even once seized the opportunity to speak of the Lord? She loved her little sister, but Euodia needed to be less concerned with what others thought of her and more outspoken for the Lord.

She pushed open the door to Cerberus's room. Propped against a pile of pillows, he stared at the far wall. She strode forward to stand at the foot of his pallet.

"Cerberus, I have a request."

He shifted his gaze to her, his face unwelcoming, his eyes shuttered.

"When you are well—and I pray you will heal completely—arrest me if you must, but spare Euodia and Brother Clement. Euodia has done nothing but try to help you, and Clement rescued you from the rats and scavengers of the back alley. You owe your life to both of them."

Syntyche waited for a nod, an indication he'd honor her request or at least consider it. Neither a flicker in his eyes nor a subtle motion of his head betrayed his thoughts.

"Very well. I will not stay today. But know this—our prayers for you will not stop when you return home. They will not stop no matter how you treat us."

She pivoted and closed the door behind her. She'd spoken to Cerberus as the Lord instructed and stopped when His words left her mind. There were others who needed to know about the Savior. She listed them in her mind: her brother, the women she worked with, strangers in the marketplace. With each step, she searched for the next person she'd be guided toward to witness to about Him—so many to speak with before her arrest.

CHAPTER TWO

Three Months Later, July

The dogs raced past, their legs moving in perfect synchronization. It was only when someone did not move out of their way fast enough that the dog in the center lifted its head and broke the illusion. In that brief flash, they appeared to be one body with three heads.

Euodia immediately thought of Cerberus and the multi-headed dog whose name he carried. In three months, there had been no word, no repercussions of witnessing to him. Each day her temper grew more brittle, her appetite dwindled, her sleep less restful. How much longer would he wait before acting against them? Would her faith withstand the humiliation of a physical punishment?

Leaving the walled city, she turned back to stare at the gate's twin towers. What would the gates of heaven be like? Not worshiping Caesar or the Roman gods could mean she saw heaven's gates sooner than she'd planned.

Not seeing Syntyche, Euodia's heart raced. Skipped a beat. Raced faster. Had the persecution begun? She pulled her linen *palla* closer around her shoulders and head—a feeble protection against danger.

She stretched her neck to search in each direction. Jostled on all sides, she moved from the traffic of the gateway to avoid being trampled. Vendors arriving for tomorrow's market day flowed around her.

Worrying her lower lip, she turned toward the meeting place. Lifting her skirts to run and warn Brother Clement of Syntyche's fate, she stopped. Pivoted toward the city gates. Helena should be warned.

"Euodia!"

At the familiar voice, relief flooded through her. Syntyche still walked free. Oblivious to the worry she'd caused, her sister rushed forward, a richly dressed woman in tow.

"Sister, this is Malitta. She is joining us for worship today. Malitta and I have been talking for several weeks."

Malitta unhooked her heavily bangled arm from Syntyche's. "So, you're Euodia, the wealthy sister who doesn't work. How clever of you to marry well."

Euodia forced a smile. This is how Syntyche thought of her?

"Euodia, hurry, now. We walk fast. Keep up with us. Brother Clement and Brother Syzygus will begin the service soon." She stopped and looked around. "Where is Helena?"

"She is unwell."

Syntyche gave a short nod. "Malitta, we meet in a house of prayer beside the river, the same spot where Lydia—you know her—the seller of purple, was baptized. Isn't that exciting? Sometimes I close my eyes and dream I'm Lydia, hearing of the

Savior—being the very first person to be baptized in the Zygakti River. Imagine being the first to know hope and salvation had come to Philippi, knowing the Light of the World had come to your own city."

Syntyche continued speaking to Malitta, but Euodia stopped listening. Slowing her steps, she trailed farther and farther behind.

Syntyche thought she didn't work? What was managing a household called? What was using her time to visit the sick and injured of the church considered? Stitching wounds or closing the eyes of those who died was not a pleasant diversion.

Euodia lifted her gaze beyond beech trees just beginning to flaunt their gold and bronze beauty. *Forgive me, Lord, for complaining about the gift You entrusted to me.*

Speeding her steps, she caught up with her sister in time for the three of them to squeeze into the women's section of the building together.

Syntyche winced when the woman in front of her trod backward on her toes. It hurt, yes, but she did not care at all. Look how many people had come to worship! Lowering her head, she was filled with praise, with exultation at the Light spreading throughout Philippi.

Joining the others, she sang praise to her Savior. A church leader read Holy Scripture, a letter from Paul to the church in Thessalonica, and prayed. Brother Clement stood to speak.

She leaned forward to hear better—and to see his eyes, the golden color of crusty bread.

He said nothing. Without moving, he stared at the back of the church.

Syzygus shuffled closer and placed his deeply veined hand on Clement's shoulder.

"Our prayers have been answered, Brother."

One by one, others turned. A murmur pulsed among the people. A groan. Then silence. Hot, dark silence—the kind too heavy to breathe.

Booted steps scraped the stone floor, carrying their owner to the front, where Clement's eyes grew wider and wider, and then, Syntyche could see what drained the color from his face.

Cerberus.

The men faced each other without speaking until Clement and Syzygus spread wide their arms and spoke words she must have misheard.

"Welcome, Brother."

The three men grasped each other's forearms before engulfing one another in a hard embrace.

"Will you allow me to address your people, Brother Clement?"

"They are yours as well. Speak as you will."

Cerberus faced the room of believers. "I am Cerberus, a believer in Jesus of Nazareth and your brother in our Lord. No longer will I oppose you."

Syntyche's lungs filled with air.

"In late March, I was attacked and left to die in the cold. By His mercy, our Lord led Brother Clement to find me. He took me to his house and sheltered me there while I healed. As I lay helpless, one of you came and shared the story of God's love." He looked around the room. "Syntyche, are you here?"

His request broke the chaste tradition of separating men and women during worship, but she wiggled through the press of women to the aisle. "Here."

Cerberus approached. She hadn't realized how tall he was.

"Syntyche, I am forever grateful to you for speaking truth I did not know I longed to hear. Your words, 'Darkness covered the souls of all people.'" He paused. Firmed his jaw. "So grateful." He swallowed. Nodded. "Thank you for your relentless determination that I know the truth. May our Lord continue to give you courage and strength to face the reluctant lost."

She grasped his hand, unable to speak.

"I came today to say thank you and farewell. I am being reassigned closer to Rome, where my commander hopes I will regain my good sense. If not, I may be joining Paul in prison." A wry smile showed his recently broken teeth. "I will not return to the worship of the gods. There is only one."

Tears blurred Syntyche's eyes. Cerberus truly loved the Lord.

He squeezed Syntyche's hands. "My sister in Christ, I pray you will remain fearless in sharing the Good News. Because of you and our Lord's mercy, perhaps I will be the kunon that guards Hades's entrance so no one enters instead of the one who guards so none can escape."

Cheers burst from the people. Cerberus nodded to the church elders and strode from the building.

A heartbeat later, both women and men surged around Syntyche. Between the hugs and shoulder pats she glimpsed Euodia leave. Why was her sister not rejoicing with everyone else or attempting to move closer so they could share a hug?

Euodia stretched her legs to their full length, taking long, hard strides. She walked as fast as she could force her legs to move. Walked without seeing where she went. Walked without swerving, turning neither left nor right. Walked until she could no longer breathe and then crumpled to the ground and sobbed.

Did her work mean nothing? Again? And yet again and again? Were her giftings, her ministry, her heart call still less valued than Syntyche's?

She'd never escape the shadow of her sister. It had hovered over her as a child and a youth. She was doomed to live beneath it forever.

Syntyche! Brilliant, vivacious Syntyche, whose flaws disappeared among the multitude of her giftings. Syntyche could sing with the angels and tempt them to sin with her cooking. She entered a room, and everyone turned with a welcoming smile. Wisdom poured forth when she opened her mouth, and when she slept she did not snore.

She was perfect, and Euodia hated her.

Torrential tears washed her face clean and cleared her mind. Calmer, she recanted her thoughts. She did not hate her sister. She loved her. Envied her. Endeavored to be like her.

And failed.

A scent-drenched hand touched her shoulder.

"Malitta!"

The woman knelt beside her—bangles clanking—and leaned close. Euodia coughed as Malitta's cloying musk filled the air.

"Dear Euodia, you have every right to be furious. After all you did for that man—Syntyche told me you saved his life—and he did not offer a word of thanks. Not one! And worse, your sister did not correct him."

Euodia shook her head. "No, it's right Cerberus thanked her. It will encourage others in the church to be bold in witnessing." Her voice rasped. Were her eyes as swollen as they felt? "I'm happy for her and proud of her. She has many gifts and is fearless in using them."

Malitta tsked. "You are so gracious, but it is shameful to be dismissed like that in front of everyone. As I was leaving, I heard Clement praised and your sister celebrated. Not a whisper from them or that older man—what's his name—of your selfless work."

"Brother Syzygus. My work is done to please the Lord. No one else's approval is needed."

"Ah." Malitta pursed her lips. "That is why you ran away and are here in the middle of"—she looked around—"nowhere." Malitta stood. "Since all is well with you, I will return to the others and join their celebration of Syntyche."

"They celebrate the Lord."

Her words scattered unheard. Malitta was nowhere to be seen.

Syntyche stood surrounded by warm smiles and joyful tears. Malitta gestured for her attention and waited until Syntyche approached.

She grasped Syntyche's upper arms and spoke in a voice that carried. "I'm so sorry to be the one to tell you, but you need to know. Euodia stomped away because she is furious no one thanked her for her work."

Syntyche recoiled from the woman as if she were a kunon. "Euodia? You must be mistaken. She's the most selfless person I know—gives with no expectation of thanks."

Malitta averted her gaze and spun the stack of bracelets circling her wrist. "She is so resentful of you, so envious."

"We could not be closer. I've watched over her like a mater since ours died." She looked over Malitta's purple-clad shoulder. "Where is she?"

"She wants time alone." Malitta twisted her lips. "She'd be terribly upset if she knew I shared with you what she said about being resentful. Maybe I shouldn't have told you."

Assuring Malitta of her silence, she ignored the surging ripples of wrongness and returned to the gathering of her friends. Malitta's report did not sound like the Euodia she knew, but it must be true. Malitta had no reason to speak falsely.

If Euodia did harbor jealousy or anger and wanted people to know the Lord, she needed to step outside herself and speak up. It was the only way.

The sun reached its zenith and began its descent before Euodia stood and brushed twigs and gravel from her clothes. Marcellus would wonder at her long absence, but she'd needed the time to cry her heart out to the Lord, time to know He heard and saw her though no one else did, and time to confess her jealousy and discontent.

No longer fueled by raging emotions and the fear her distress would be observed, Euodia's return to the church took much longer than it had earlier. She paused by the river, swatted at the humming mosquitos, and washed her face in its cool clearness before continuing to the city gates.

Late-arriving vendors from neighboring villages crowded the Naples Gate, but she slipped past them into the city, crossed the road separating the city in half, the Via Egnatia, and stole through the stone paved streets to her home. Feet dragging, she stepped into her deserted atrium and sighed with relief. Her lateness might go unnoticed.

Something—a heavy sigh, the scrape of a chair, or maybe the force of his displeasure—alerted her. She looked beyond the shallow pool.

Marcellus watched her from his office. The set of his jaw warned her he was not happy.

Trying to add spring to her steps, she hurried toward him, circling the shallow pool—and stumbled. His scowl lifted. He grasped her elbow, leading her to a seat and settling her against the cushions. He eased the palla from her shoulders and draped it behind her.

"I was worried."

"Marcellus, I'm sorry. I went to worship and became"—she searched for a word he'd accept—"distracted. It was thoughtless of me. Forgive me and tell me about the meeting."

"Have you eaten?"

"I'm not hungry."

Against her protests, Marcellus called to a servant and ordered food and drink be prepared for her.

She tucked her feet beneath her and reached for his hand. "While we wait, please tell me of your day. Did the meeting go as you hoped? Will they display your sculptures? What about your paintings? I hope you mentioned you paint as well."

Marcellus flicked his hand in dismissal. "Later. First, we discuss you and your new God. He and His followers demand too much of you."

She shook her head in denial, but his fingers touched the skin beneath her eyes.

"These circles darken, and today they are puffy as if you've been crying."

At times, his artist eyes missing nothing was a problem.

"You know how much I sneeze this time of year."

"Euodia."

The flatness of his voice warned her he did not believe her excuse.

"Yes, I have been crying. It has nothing to do with my Lord and everything to do with my sister." She brushed an invisible strand of hair from her forehead, attempting to look nonchalant. "It is a sister problem. You know I love her, but sometimes she is…Syntyche."

"This is not the first time she's said something to upset you."

"She said nothing to upset me. I did not like how she handled a situation and reacted poorly to it. Honestly, she had little control over the matter. It no longer concerns me."

She forced a smile. Marcellus's expression revealed he questioned her words, but he did not push her to share more.

"Euodia, I know you're tired, but there is another matter I've waited all day to share with you." He reached for a bowl of grapes and popped one in her mouth. "My parents."

She swallowed the grape whole.

"Remember when they built a new estate on the property from Tiberius Caesar and then gave us this house as a wedding gift? We promised they could always return here if needed."

She remembered it well. Some of the farmers Tiberius rashly displaced with his careless deeds had been believers. They'd lost their homes of countless generations and been forced to find refuge in the city as menial laborers.

At her nod, he continued. "*Pater*'s war wound still bothers him. Mater says he wants to be closer to town for frequent medical care, but I think they miss visiting with their friends. Since they gave us this house, it seems only right they remain here as long as necessary."

Euodia kept her face smooth, her spine straight. She breathed steadily. She tucked her trembling hands beneath her skirts and remained seated, not trusting her legs to support her weight.

"Of course, Marcellus—as long as necessary."

Inwardly, she wept. Marcellus's parents alternated between scolding their gods for disappointing them with their only child's choice of wife and reminding her the gods favored her since Marcellus had married beneath himself with the youngest child of a Greek merchant.

Dear Lord, will he ever belong to You if his parents are here to sway him?

She glanced at Marcellus. Had he caught her biting her lip and realized her distress at his news?

"They will bring their collection of board games. You enjoy those, don't you, Euodia? And their friends will often be here. I expect they will bring servants with them. Do you think you'll need more servants?"

"No." She needed a quiet, peaceful home.

She'd never traveled to the great city, but his parents, Atticus and Amelia, must be more Roman than Rome, extolling its virtues increasingly with each year despite their exile—a generous but decreed exile. She thought it odd the way Tiberius compensated those who'd fought for him. The Rome they praised seemed like a vicious, violent city to her, but maybe being a veteran inured one to the bloodthirsty sports Atticus recounted. How Amelia stomached it she did not understand.

"Euodia." Tension clipped the edge of his words. "You know they neither accept nor approve of your new religion."

A deep breath allowed her to speak without rancor. "I neither accept nor approve of theirs."

"Do not provoke them or speak of your beliefs. I could command you as most husbands do their wives, but I'd rather have your promise that you will not become like Syntyche while they are with us."

She hesitated—too long, from the alarm in his eyes. Maybe Syntyche's frequent admonitions were right—as usual—and she should be bold in speaking of the Lord. Something inside her cringed. She could never be so outspoken. Euodia lifted her chin enough that Marcellus would see her determination. "I will not be my sister, but I will be me and not who your parents want me to be."

Resignation shadowed his eyes, but he pulled her out of the chair and into his embrace.

"Be careful, my beloved. Remember my pater was a praetorian guard. As an elite guard to the emperor, he still has strong connections in Rome. If his guard friends realize you do not worship Caesar, we could lose everything—even each other."

CHAPTER THREE

August

Buoyed by last month's encounter with Cerberus, Syntyche hummed as she balanced the wooden tray of breads and pastries on her head. The warm, buttery fragrance of freshly baked goods wafting down to tease her nose tempted her to reach up and snatch a pastry for herself. She didn't. These delicacies were promised to Albus, the manager of the most popular bath, who offered them to his clients as complimentary refreshments and incentive to patronize only his bath. His patrons relished her sweet breads, savory spinach pies oozing with cheese, crispy baklava, and syrup cakes.

With one hand, she touched the coin purse hidden in the folds of her clothes. With not a single copper coin, it was as empty as her food bins and lamp wells. Today, she'd be paid and paid well. This was the fourth time this week she'd walked the Via Egnatia through the city to deliver the sweet indulgences.

Thankfully, Albus knew her reputation as the finest baker in the city and, as an incentive to provide goods only for his establishment, allowed her to use the baths at no charge. It saved her precious coins to buy more ingredients.

Syntyche entered through the front door, the ones the patrons used. Not a servant's entrance for her. She might be a servant to Albus, but she was a daughter of Almighty God.

She lowered the wooden tray from her head onto the table reserved for her goods, shook off the hood of her linen palla, and rubbed the kinks from her neck.

Before she could remove her palla, she was surrounded by those eager to have first choice of the still-warm breads and cakes. Delighted, she laughed. "This is how eager you should be to know of my Lord Jesus."

One person winked, another gave a discreet nod, and a few laughed with her. Some touched her shoulder or squeezed her hand—all believers she had shared the Good News with here at the baths.

Others snatched their treat and scurried away. She was left facing Mania, Albus's wife or mater. She'd never been sure if Albus had married a much older woman or if he lived with his mater. It would be embarrassing to ask so late in their relationship.

Mania tilted her head down, doubling her chin. "You have said this before to our patrons. I've heard you, as have others. Exactly who is this Lord Jesus?"

Syntyche beckoned her to a quiet niche and leaned against a stone ledge. "I will tell you all I know so you may know Him too. Jesus is a real person and the true God. In some ways He is like you and me."

Mania's eyebrows rose a tiny bit.

"When I was a child and afraid of the night shadows, I'd call out and my mater would hurry to comfort me, to banish the mysteries of the darkness with her lighted lamp. She rescued me whenever I needed her, and I loved her for it."

She grinned, hoping to find common ground and set the woman at ease. "When you were young, were you ever afraid of the dark and its mysteries? Did you cry out for someone to come with a light and drive the scaries away?"

Mania stared at her.

Inwardly, Syntyche chuckled. A dead fish stare would not dissuade her. "Mania, there is a darkness blacker and deeper than the night, a darkness covering the souls of all people. Fathomless darkness…" She told the story, thankful to be able to share. "…a yearning for light. The Creator God knew we wandered in despair, heard our cry of fear, saw our helplessness, and sent a Savior."

"Like Caesar, who brought salvation here to Macedonia."

"Mmmm." Syntyche squelched a denial. Instead, she leaned closer, eager to share her experience. "From my youth, I have excelled at all I set my hand to do. As an adult, I believed I no longer needed rescuing from anything or anyone, yet I did. Let me tell you my story."

Mania crossed her arms, her demeanor belligerent.

Syntyche understood. Her own first reaction when hearing she needed a savior had been red anger born of fear, of humiliation at her inadequacy, of shame spreading like deadly mold.

"Day by day, I became increasingly aware I could not meet my own standards much less a god's demands. No matter how I entreated the gods—"

Mania uncrossed one arm and shook her finger. "It is better to choose and serve only one or two—three at the most. It flatters them, and they will answer you more favorably."

Syntyche ignored the interruption. "I believed the gods not only turned from me, they also turned on me. I lost almost everything dear to me. Our business failed, and my husband died not long after the death of our only child."

Mania shuddered and shrank away. At the familiar response, Syntyche knew that since her listener feared being contaminated by one who incurred the displeasure and wrath of the gods, she'd really be offended by the next part of the story.

"Pain engulfed me until I could neither speak nor weep. I could not eat or sleep, only breathe—and that was with grueling effort." She drew in a long breath and slowly released it to steady herself. This part hurt to remember.

"Living without my husband and child was inconceivable." She looked beyond Mania into the past. "Grief is grueling, exhausting—every thought an ache, every memory a dagger, an open wound. I could not live in such wretchedness."

Her focus returned to the present and she met Mania's gaze. "I determined to end the excruciating pain and take my life."

She gasped, the double chins wobbling. "Shame on you."

"By God's grace, my sister realized what I intended and refused to leave me alone. I ignored her, turned my back, rejected her words, refused to respond, but she forced me to listen to her. She told me over and over about Jesus, Son of the one, true God, the Savior and solace she knew I desperately needed. Finally, I listened." Syntyche dashed away tears and smiled. "Jesus has become everything to me."

"You are a widow, yes? Is this your lover?"

Syntyche laughed and dipped her head. "In a way, yes. Lover of my soul. God Himself become human."

Mania drew herself up and back—a coiled snake ready to strike. "You say your lover is a god?"

Syntyche ignored the warning of the still voice inside her. "Jesus is God Incarnate. He is living inside me through the Holy Spirit."

"Your lover is a god, and a spirit lives inside you. I see."

Syntyche tensed. Why did this woman insist on twisting her words?

Mania looked upward and tapped one finger against her lips. "Is this a spirit like the one in the slave girl a few years ago? She foretold the future until some Jew interfered—a traveling tradesman."

"You speak of Paul, who freed her from a demonic spirit. This is God's spirit, not an evil one."

"Your thoughts and actions are controlled by this spirit?"

Syntyche fanned herself. The steam rising from the bathing rooms seemed unusually warm. "The Holy Spirit guides me, but I choose whether to obey."

Mania gestured toward the acropolis crowning Mount Orvelos. "Do you honor our ancestors? Do you give fealty to our gods? Worship in their temples? Bring them offerings?"

Syntyche looked into the woman's small eyes without hesitation. "Once I gave tribute to Hera —"

"As do I. Well, I worship Juno." She shrugged. "Hera—Juno, they are the same. One Greek, one Roman. Goddess of marriage and queen of the gods. A worthy choice." Mania nodded approval.

Syntyche held up a hand to interrupt Mania. "But no longer do I worship her. She, like all the others, are not true gods, merely stone figures someone chiseled from boulders."

She gasped. The double chins became three. "This spirit that possesses you has led you to denounce the ancient gods who have protected us throughout the years."

Syntyche subdued a smirk but not her retort. "Protected us? Then how is it we have been beneath Roman rule for almost two centuries?"

If the woman had had feathers, she'd have ruffled them. "Tell me you at least worship the emperor, Nero. He too has brought us peace."

"Never."

"You confess you are a traitor as well as a blasphemer."

"I do not." Syntyche drew back from the pointed finger inches from her face. "I confess I am a follower of the Lord Jesus Christ."

"And you need never return to this establishment."

Syntyche, startled by the voice from behind her, whirled and gaped at Albus.

"I will find a new baker. We don't want your kind here." Albus dropped a pouch of coins into her lap. "We are finished.

You offend my patrons' ears with lies and abuse the privilege of serving here. I will tolerate it no longer."

Chills shot from her scalp, along her shoulders, and through her stomach to weaken her knees. Wide-eyed, she searched for a trace of the lopsided smile revealing he was not serious. Against her will, her lips trembled and curved downward. She fought against doubling over as knots wrenched her stomach into a ball.

Unfair! Mania had *asked* her to share—had approached and questioned her. Seeing the woman's gloat and Albus's set jaw, she swallowed, her throat so taut, the swallow hurt. Protests or explanations would go unheard.

Mania's sneer goaded her to action. Scooping up the pouch, Syntyche weighed it in her hand and jutted out her chin. "You owe me four days, not two."

Albus scowled and slung a second bag of coins to the floor. "We are done. Leave through the back door, the latrine door. We don't want to be associated with you and your absurd, deceitful beliefs. Be assured you'll never find work anywhere in this city again."

Syntyche snatched the purse and rose to stand on trembling legs. She marched to the front entrance, opened it, and looked over her shoulder. "I will pray for you and your mater or wife or whoever Mania is to you."

"My daughter!"

The indignation in Albus's voice pleased her, though she knew it should not have.

Stepping away from the entrance to the building, she stared at the enormous theater across the street. She'd heard it was similar to the Coliseum in Rome, though smaller. Unsurprising since they served the same purpose—glorifying the emperor—and today, Rome, or its goddess, Juno, had won a battle at the baths.

Shoulders starting to droop, she chided herself. "Remember the One you serve—the One who defeated death. Let Rome have its little victory." Only it wasn't a little victory. It was two souls snared by lies and the lost opportunity to share the love of Jesus with the people she met at the baths.

Spying a tall woman with a brilliant purple head covering, she panicked. Malitta! Before the woman could turn and see her, Syntyche pivoted and bolted around the corner onto a street running parallel to Via Egnatia. Going against her nature, she wanted to avoid familiar faces in the crowded marketplace today. Shops lined this way also, but if she kept her head down and moved without pausing, perhaps no one would recognize her and call out to gesture her closer for a visit. She needed to be home—alone—with time to think, to pray, to surrender this hardship to the Lord.

Walking quickly, she moved past the busy commerce part of town and closer to the residential area. Winding through narrow streets lined with modest houses, she sighed in relief at the sight of her cozy ownness—a solace, a haven—the home where she'd lived with her husband and they'd grieved the loss of their only child, a girl who breathed just once—long enough to capture and fracture their hearts. When Alex died, she'd comforted herself by imagining their child, Lily, nestling against him, the delicate creaminess of her impossibly small body in stark contrast to his sun-roughened skin. The thought brought solace as no words ever had. Time had eased the intensity of loss—not her awareness of it.

Five steps covered the length of her yard with its evergreen olive tree. Safe. She leaned her head against the wooden door. Home.

Here, she'd grieved and healed—survived. Here she'd honed her kitchen skills and begun the business that allowed her to remain independent instead of returning home to live beneath her older brother's authority. Here too she'd learned to pray and trust the Lord.

So much joy lost—husband, child, business—and likely now, her independence. Kitchen skills granted her freedom. Faith gave her a future. She held both closely. They defined her life.

Unlocking the door, she inhaled the sweet remnants of browned butter and roasted nuts, of baked bread and cinnamon. Bunched on the table was a wet cloth she'd forgotten to hang up. Across the back of a chair draped a blanket Mater had given her.

Slipping her sandals off, she curled her bare toes against the uneven stone floor. She shivered despite the day's warmth, removed her palla, and hung it on a hook by the door. Emotion overwhelming her, she buried her face in the comfort of its rumpled coarseness.

Without her only weekly income, she'd lose this house, this sanctuary of memories. Fear threatened to choke her, and she clung to the palla as if it were her Lord Himself.

Knots clenched her stomach. Bile rose in her throat. Tears burned her eyes and streamed down her cheeks. Strength drained from her arms. Releasing the palla, she crumpled to the floor.

No longer able to bear the fear, the discouragement alone, she felt her pain well and spill—her heart's plea desperate. "Help me. Help me. Help me."

Infinitesimally, the storm calmed. Peace surrounded, warmed her. Her breathing steadied. Her mind cleared.

The room remained dark, the floor cold, her larder empty, but the sharp aching in her throat eased though her voice rasped hoarse. "The Lord is my shepherd.... He leads me.... He restores me.... I will fear no evil for He is with me. He is with me. He is. With me."

A knowing of His presence swept through her.

A knowing He would bring good from this.

A knowing she was cherished.

Syntyche pushed herself to stand. She wobbled to the table, shook out the wadded cloth, and hung it to dry. In spite of the warm, humid night, she wrapped herself in the comfort of her mater's warm blanket, curled onto her bed, and slept.

Morning came softly. She opened swollen eyes to sparkling dust stars dancing through the early light. Sitting up, she stretched the tightness from her shoulders, yawned—and remembered.

The dust no longer sparkled or danced. It dulled the air, stifling her breath. Heart as heavy as one of the marble plinths lining the streets, she crossed her legs and dropped her chin in her hands.

If only someone was here to reassure her, to carry this burden with her. Someone she could talk to and confess she was afraid but knew the Lord was with her, someone to understand, like Alex or Mater, both passed from this world—or Euodia.

She snorted.

Euodia would never understand. She'd never be in this situation. Nothing was ever difficult for her. Married into wealth, Euodia's every wish was granted. Her sister's clothes were the finest, her perfumes delicate, her home spacious and beautiful with enough servants to ensure it ran effortlessly. Euodia did nothing but visit a few of the sick believers and attend parties with her wealthy friends.

"Paul would be so disappointed in her." She sniffed. "If he only knew how little she does for our Lord, he'd have something to say to her. Maybe Clement should correct her."

Syntyche tilted her head remembering. At first, as new believers and before Euodia married Marcellus, they'd worked side by side, witnessing to the women they knew as Paul mended tents and spoke to those who needed his skill.

"At least I witnessed." She crossed her arms. "Come to think of it, Euodia never said much. I took the risk. Telling the story, being spat upon, revealing the lowest moment of my life and the difference Jesus brought to my life. I even introduced Paul to many of the people."

True, Euodia cared for infants and prepared the deceased for burial, but any woman could do that. It was the telling others about Jesus that was so important.

"Euodia would never be in my situation because she is too timid. She's a mouse—always has been even as a child."

She squashed the memory of Euodia pleading with her to be sensitive to those she spoke to about Jesus. This was life or death. They should be told whether they wished to hear it or not.

"Paul commended me for my work. I wonder if he ever commended Euodia for anything. Poor little thing. I guess she tries." Syntyche sighed. "I'll just leave her to the Lord."

Syntyche washed her face and hands, knowing she'd miss the free baths and long, warm soaks. Dressing herself in a clean linen *stola*, she soothed her growling stomach with a drink of water and knelt to pray.

"You are all I have, Lord. The only One who knows all, who can guide me. Help me, please, for Your Son's sake. Amen."

She rejected the thought when it first came. There must be another way than returning home to live with her brother. He'd grown from a gentle child into a difficult man. But he did like to eat, and she could cook, and he knew it. He'd take her in.

Still, it was not a good plan.

She waited for a different answer to her prayer, and when it didn't come, she explained its unsuitability to the Almighty.

"Lord, this won't work. Tymon is not a believer in You or any god—Greek, Roman, or otherwise. He believes in himself, his value, his skills, his determination. He's not going to *approve* of me returning home, even if he allows it."

She'd wait as long as it took. Surely the Lord would reconsider and provide another solution.

Euodia stepped over olives littering Syntyche's yard. She liked to eat olives. Happily, she did not need to grow them. If cutting an olive tree down was not a crime punishable by death, she'd coax her sister to have it removed. Ripening olives were such a mess. She tsked. Poor Syntyche to live in such a tiny house jammed against other tiny houses with only a single puny tree for shade.

Standing outside her sister's door, she fidgeted with the brooch pinned to her mantle, shifted the basket of baked goods to the other arm, and cleared her throat.

"Knock and go inside," she prompted herself. Her whisper echoed loudly in the morning's quiet. "It's early, but she's your sister and the Lord told you to come here."

Still, she hesitated. "Lord, why am I here? Syntyche doesn't need me. She's the strong one, the smart one. Besides, she's going to badger me about leaving the worship service after Cerberus's testimony." She turned to leave.

"I don't want to hear it nor explain myself." Syntyche's glorification still smarted as it had since Euodia was a child growing up in her sister's shadow, knowing she'd never excel the way her older siblings did.

She glanced at the heavens. "I do not want to be here, but You led me, so I'll greet her and leave."

Raising her arm, she fisted her hand then drew it back to her chest. The longer she waited, the larger the door loomed and the more certain she grew of an unwelcome reception.

She'd just leave the basket on the step. Syntyche would know who brought it because it held her favorites.

"If she truly needs me, she'll come to my house."

Knock. An invisible force lifted her fist to the door. She knocked.

Syntyche opened the door. Euodia wasn't sure who was more surprised—Syntyche at seeing her there or herself at seeing Syntyche's puffy, reddened eyes. Without a word, Euodia stepped inside, let the basket tumble to the floor, and embraced her sister with both arms.

When Syntyche finally pulled away, Euodia bent down to scoop up the basket.

"Hungry?" She crossed to the table, noticing no fruit or breads filled the bowls on the shelves. With a flourish, she presented the pastries she'd spread on a linen cloth. "These aren't as good as yours or the ones Mater used to bake, but they'll have to do. I didn't think to bring fruit."

Syntyche pinched off a corner of a croissant. "How did you know?"

"Know?"

"I no longer work for Albus. He plans to find another baker."

Breath whooshed from Euodia. "You quit?" Quitting was an unknown concept to Syntyche except that once, when mourning the death of her family. Euodia shuddered, remembering how she'd almost lost her sister.

"He insisted." Syntyche tore another piece from the croissant and shredded it. "Ordered me to leave by the latrine door."

Euodia gasped. "You didn't."

"I didn't." She crumbled the shred into pieces. "Mania, his daughter—I'll tell you about that later—asked me about Jesus and then took offense. She wanted Him to be just another stone figure and became upset when informed I once worshiped Hera, but now I worship none of the Twelve Olympians, nor even Rome's Caesar." She pursed her lips. "Thinking back, I realize Mania was determined to be upset before I shared. Her questions were strange too. I think she intended to be offended."

The sisters' gaze locked with understanding. Lost opportunity, lost souls, a tarnished reputation, all forerunners of more loss.

"Your house?"

"I have enough coins for one more month." Syntyche rolled her eyes. "If I don't eat."

"What will you do?"

Syntyche stood and paced the room. "Cling to the Lord, pray for guidance, and"—her voice wobbled—"maybe move."

"Brother Clement might help—"

"No. Don't you dare."

"I'll speak with Marcellus. We can afford to—"

"Never."

"You could stay with us. I'm sure Marcellus won't mind, although his parents will be living with us for a while. It's a big house." Euodia bit her tongue.

"No."

Euodia raised her hands in frustration. "Then how do I help you?"

"Pray with me. I asked our Lord to lead me, but so far there's been no answer—not one that works."

Euodia narrowed her eyes. "What unworkable answer did He send?"

"Tymon."

"Our brother Tymon? Oh, Syntyche, that's…hard. Maybe it was a different Tymon."

"I know two others by that name, but one is an infant and the other moved away several years ago."

The sisters sat in silence—Syntyche motionless, Euodia twitching her foot in agitation.

At last, Euodia sighed and stood. "Marcellus's parents arrive today. I'm sorry not to stay longer, but I need to be home to welcome them, and before I return, I want to check on the baby I tended yesterday. I'll be praying for you to know if Tymon is the Lord's answer."

With a quick hug, Euodia gathered her things and closed the door softly behind her. She walked home, eyes downcast. She hurt for Syntyche, but if her sister was not so bold, if she could approach witnessing with more delicacy, she'd still have her job, her house, and the opportunity to show Jesus's love to the masses who used the baths. Instead, she'd thrown it all away.

Had Syntyche seen relief in her eyes when the offer to live with her and Marcellus was rejected? A sincere offer and Marcellus would have graciously—though reluctantly—welcomed her. Still, it would have been uncomfortable with Atticus and Amelia opposed to her faith and Syntyche's outspoken promotion of it. Their brother would oppose Syntyche also.

Tymon and Syntyche. She shuddered. Lavender and garlic. Cilantro and dill. Basil and cloves. Each good on their own. Disastrous when combined.

CHAPTER FOUR

Euodia rubbed the back of her neck. Her day had not improved. She'd returned to Atticus's and Amelia's furniture and trunks of clothes cluttering the atrium. Linus, her white Maltese, voiced displeasure with every bark. Her servants squabbled with the newly arrived servants, and her cook—almost as good as Syntyche—threatened to quit if she had to share the kitchen. Marcellus was nowhere to be seen. Her sister's quiet house, instead of being lowly and sparse, seemed like a retreat from chaos.

Euodia cornered one of the new arrivals, an older servant. "When do our guests arrive?"

He shrugged. "They were not awake when we left the estate."

Good. That gave her half a morning to sort and settle the ruckus.

She clapped her hands and spoke sharply. "Felix, Anna, Claudia, attend me now. Doris, catch Linus and bring him here."

Tripping over the boxes and bags, they hurried forward seeming ready for direction in the chaos.

"Doris, gather the female servants. I counted eleven—who needs so many? Tell them to follow you with their belongings and take them to the room on the left at the back."

She looked into Felix's rheumy eyes. "I forbid you to lift a single box. You are to direct the male servants as they carry the furniture to the room we prepared. Once everything is cleared away, show them to their quarters.

"Anna, assure the cook no one enters her domain without her approval. She'll listen to you. When she's calm, return to me for more instructions. And Anna, remind her refreshments must be available as soon as our guests arrive.

"Claudia, when the women are settled, send them to prepare our guests' room as they prefer it. They may not rest nor take refreshment until it is complete, no matter how they whine."

Gentling her voice, she stepped closer to them. "What would I do without such capable people as you?"

Euodia lifted her chin and swept from the room. If the new people saw she trusted her servants and expected orders to be followed, they'd be quicker to obey. Out of sight, she slumped against a wall and buried her face in Linus's fur. Four servants and a cook and kitchen boy were all the household help she could manage. What was she to do with eleven more servants, condescending in-laws, and the remaining baggage and attendants they'd bring?

"Mistress?"

Euodia bolted upright and away from the wall. Had Anna seen her lapse into weakness? Did her lips twist in a smirk?

"Mistress, while I was speaking with Cook, a message arrived from a woman named Helena. She said she is not ill nor is Clement, but she wishes to speak with you as soon as you can manage it."

"Order the two-mule *cisium* to be readied immediately—the smallest one."

"Yes, mistress." Anna rolled her lips inward as if to prevent more words from spilling out.

Euodia looked at her uncertainly.

"I'll be home soon. It's a visit of mercy." She stopped. It was unnecessary to explain her decisions. "It is imperative my husband receive that message."

Imagining reproof in Anna's eyes, she started to cancel the directive. Anna was right. She was leaving before all was settled and when honored guests were expected. Within an hour, she'd be discussed and dissected by the servants. They'd rebel, reveal their disrespect in subtle ways. Marcellus would hear of it. Her in-laws would notice or be informed by their servants of her irresponsibility. They'd scold her—in front of the servants or wealthy guests, and she'd never be accepted by—

Lord, I'm doing it again. She inhaled deeply. Exhaled. *What do You want me to do?*

By the time the small carriage rolled in front of the entrance, Euodia had surrendered a reluctant Linus to the kitchen boy's care, clasped her palla around her shoulders, and retrieved a small medical box. No matter Helena said they were not ill—it was better to be prepared for the worst. If she hurried, she might also have time to deliver medicine to the cousin of a new believer.

She settled against the pillows and grasped the side strap preparing for the carriage's lurch as it moved forward. Helena did not live too far, but this was quicker than walking, and if the dear woman was still unwell—she'd been sick on worship day—she could care for her sooner.

She owed so much to Helena, bringer of light, like her name.

The cisium jolted to a stop. She directed the driver to wait and let herself in Helena's front door, knowing she'd be scolded if she didn't. Helena regarded her as the daughter she never had. The house still smelled of quince. Euodia inhaled the fragrance, feeling her tension ease and her spirits rise at being able to visit with her friend. A servant greeted her and led her to the garden where Helena waited.

"I knew you'd come right away." Helena patted the seat next to her. "It's urgent we talk."

Euodia set her medicine box on the floor. "Are you hurting? Ill?" The woman's color was weak, and she looked as if she'd not been eating.

"Not as you mean, my dear. I am sick at heart and hurting for you."

Euodia stopped evaluating Helena's health and stared into her eyes. "I don't understand."

"Last worship. Cerberus."

"Oh." Euodia looked down and poked the medical box with her toes.

"It should never have happened. Inexcusable. A terrible occurrence."

Euodia touched Helena's hand. "I have taken it to the Lord, and He is healing my hurt."

At Helena's puzzlement she continued. "He's reminding me I serve to honor Him, not for personal glory."

The older woman blinked. Her lips parted and closed.

"Truly, Helena, it is of no consequence, but I am so grateful for your concern."

"Your hurt?" Helena shook her head as if to clear her thoughts. "Do you not know, or do you not care, that your sister was distressed, deeply hurt by your snub? How could you leave without speaking to her, rejoicing with her?"

Flustered, Euodia pulled her hand away. "She was hurt? We spoke this morning, and she said nothing." She shook her head. "No, Helena, you are mistaken. We are sisters. If we misstep, we speak openly with each other, forgive, and move on. We do not allow ill feelings to linger between us."

"Not this time. Syntyche was warned not to reveal she knew of your anger and bitterness. Others, also, heard how you resent not being publicly thanked for helping with Cerberus. If Christ-following sisters cannot live in harmony..."

Warned by who? She'd said nothing to anyone. Malitta had followed her, but she'd not shared anything with that woman. Maybe someone noticed her countenance before she had time to escape and hide herself.

Helena frowned. "Dear, selfishness is not the way we as Christ followers are called to live. You and your sister must work together in unity. If you demand to be praised for everything you do, it will lead to bitterness and destroy the work Paul and Clement have done."

Demand to be praised? Euodia's head spun at the double slap of injustice and realization that Helena's summons was to chide her—not to comfort her nor out of personal need.

Shame burned her face. Others discussed and criticized her, and, worse, there was a bit of truth in their censure—she did want others to notice her efforts for the Lord.

She served the other believers with her husband's reluctant consent but not his approval. She paid for the medicines with her money and gave her time several days a week to comfort the sick and listen to the sick at heart. No one praised her. Ever.

Tears spilled from her eyes, scalding her cheeks. She dashed at the tears, mortified when they refused to stop.

It was too much. Cerberus, Syntyche, her in-laws, Anna, and now, Helena. Ugly sobs tore through her throat, wracking her body. She jerked her hand from Helena's cool touch and covered her face.

A linen cloth was pressed into her hand. Vaguely, she heard Helena fretting, cajoling her to stop crying.

"Please, Euodia. I know you are contrite. Do not punish yourself like this. I'm sure you and Syntyche can restore harmony. Please, stop. My dear, I never supposed you'd be so upset."

Euodia's head throbbed, but her tears slowly eased. A dry cloth replaced the sopping one and Euodia scrubbed the remaining moisture from her face. She did not look at Helena. She turned away when a servant girl approached.

"Mistress Helena, a messenger has come for your guest. He said she is needed at home. Her in-laws have arrived."

Euodia closed her eyes, fighting the tears' return. She refused to humiliate herself further. Losing the battle, she buried her face in her hands, her features crumpling behind their finger shield.

How wrong she'd been to come here, leaving her home in chaos, risking Marcellus's parents' early arrival. Marcellus would be disappointed in her. Helena was disappointed. Paul would be disappointed. Her fellow believers were probably disappointed. Jesus was—

You cannot disappoint Me. I know your weaknesses and needs.

He'd led her here today knowing what the visit held.

Lord, why?

Trust Me.

Her breath steadied. Tears still burned her eyes, but they no longer ran down her face. She lifted her medical box and stood.

"Thank you for your concern." She could not bring herself to say the name of the one before her. "As you heard, I must leave immediately." With a quick dip of her head, she walked to the front door.

Helena trailed behind her. "We will talk later, dear."

Outside, Euodia squinted as sun shards pierced her tear-soaked eyes. The ride home proved too short for her eyes to lose their puffiness but long enough for her to calm herself—outwardly. Within, she reeled from her "visit of mercy." Only the Lord's *Trust Me* soothed her.

After rearranging the folds of her stola, she straightened the pendant at her throat, fanned her cheeks, and moistened her lips. She'd expected to apply light makeup before her guests arrived. Amelia, always impeccable, would comment on any sign of disarray. Emotional displays were intolerable and to be ignored.

The carriage halted. Squaring her shoulders, Euodia stepped down and swept into her home. She unfastened the brooch of her palla before releasing the mantle into Claudia's waiting arms. She replaced her sandals with soft house shoes.

Atticus's stiff greeting and Amelia's chilly smile were expected. Marcellus's worried expression was not.

"Is all well?" His artist eyes scrutinized her face. Did tear lines streak her face?

"I thought my presence was urgently needed, or I'd never have left knowing that your parents arrived today." Did he hear the tremble in her voice? Did hurt lace her tones? "I'm sorry this has caused distress for you and discomfort for them."

"As long as you are well."

Tears welled again at the tenderness of his concern. Unable to speak, she nodded and turned to her in-laws.

"Pater Atticus, Mater Amelia, please join me in the gardens for refreshment. I hope it will be to your liking and that you will forgive the delay in hospitality."

Amelia looked pointedly at Euodia's flat stomach. "Another delay among many." She sniffed. "We've learned to expect disappointment from you."

Euodia refused to wilt or cower. Too much had happened today. Tears hedged the past. Defiance endangered the future. Fuming, she turned on her heel and led the way, her short, quick steps soundless on the mosaic floor. If she'd been wearing sandals, the staccato slap would have betrayed her frustration. *Lord, overshadow me so You are seen and not me.*

CHAPTER FIVE

September

Not enough. Not even a full day's wage. Syntyche counted the coins again and lined up the ten little copper images of Nike, goddess of victory. She flipped to the Latin words on the other side. *Cohor. Prae. Phil.* Praetorian Cohorts of Philippi. Another reminder that Philippi was overrun with Praetorian veterans.

Returning to the loose stone that had hidden her small horde, she wiggled her fingers into each corner searching for overlooked coins. Nothing.

"Lord? I'm listening, still waiting for your answer."

Tymon.

She groaned. The same wrong answer every time she asked. Returning home to live under her brother's control was humiliating as well as annoying. He'd been opposed to her living alone and supporting herself and warned her she'd fail.

She counted the coins again. Still not enough. Ty was right. She failed. He'd gloat.

"Lord, what am I going to do?"

Tymon.

"Fine." The coins bounced as she slapped her hands on the table. She'd go to her brother. Ty would take her in. It would be a disaster. Maybe then the Lord would give her a different answer.

Pushing away from the table, she gathered empty food storage boxes and baskets and began to fill them with her cooking wares, stuffing pillows and linens between them for protection.

She had little else of value—her mater's blanket, a few clothes, a wooden spice and herb box that Alex had bought for her, a rattle he'd carved for their infant, the doll she'd secretly sewn in hope of a baby girl to name after her mater. A plant from Mater's garden and the oil lamp she'd bought with her first earnings completed her packing.

She'd scoured the table, scrubbing away every evidence of her baking business but not the memories of women gathered around it learning her baking secrets as she imbued each lesson with Jesus's teachings. Jana, Chloe, Sophia, and Zoe—how would they continue to learn of the Lord since each was forbidden to attend the church?

The floor was swept. An earring found. A delicate spiderweb disturbed.

The mattress and bed remained for the next owner. There was no need for her to take the furniture. Ty had kept intact the room she and Euodia had shared when they lived at home.

Her pile of belongings stacked against the wall, she snuggled into her palla, tugged the door closed, and began to trudge home—no, to Tymon's house. This was home.

She did not cry. It was the wind that whipped tears into her eyes.

Ty was not home when she arrived. So much the better. She traipsed around the side of the house and entered through the back and into the kitchen. Draping her palla across a low stool, she dismissed the kitchen servants, pushed the sleeves of her stola past her elbows, and began gathering flour, eggs, spices, and butter.

Two hours later, the kitchen smelled of cinnamon and yeast. She pressed the balls of her palms into the third mound of floured dough. Push. Pull. Push. Pull. Fold. Flip. Push. The rhythmic kneading, as familiar as breathing, eased her tension.

Maybe the Lord was right.

Ty liked to eat. She liked to cook and bake. Living with her brother, she could witness to him every day. The Lord would bring good through Rome's little victory. If—no, *when* Ty became a believer, their entire family could work together for the Lord. Well, except Marcellus, who still followed the Roman gods. Euodia needed to be more direct in witnessing to her husband. If she'd be bolder—

"Synee."

Tymon leaned against the doorframe, unsmiling. Was he annoyed to find her in his kitchen?

Heart racing, she searched his face for the signs Euodia said revealed he was upset. His jaw did not twitch. His hands remained still and unclenched. Frown lines did not crease his forehead. And yet his eyes were shuttered.

"Why are you here? Tell me."

Answers flooded her mind. *"I missed you." "I wanted to surprise you." "Hello to you too."* He knew her too well, would know she lied.

She spoke truth, waited for him to gloat. "I lost my job and the house."

"I heard." His gaze softened. "I'm sorry, Synee. More loss in your life. What happened?"

"I spoke of the Lord Jesus to one who did not truly want to know of Him." She brushed flour from her hands. "The coins I earned are spent, and no one will hire me for fear of offending Albus and being refused entrance to the bath. I have nowhere to go. May I return home?"

His eyes flickered. Anger? Dismay? Resentment?

"You have to ask? Synee, you are my family. Of course you can come home. I expected you sooner."

She released a long breath. Hurt! He was hurt she hadn't turned to him earlier.

"However"—Ty pushed away from the door and lines marred his forehead—"I refuse to be plagued with this Jesus talk in my own home. Do not bring those Jews or Jesus people or anyone else here. I will not be badgered about your new religion."

"It's not a religion, it's a relationship with—"

"Synee, stop." The muscles in his jaw tightened. "Keep it to yourself. I'm not interested. Try to be like Euodia. Do you hear me?"

She sank her hands into the dough. Push. Pull. Push. Raising her head, she glared at him. He glared back.

"I hear you."

"Good. I'll have my steward send someone for your things." He tore off a chunk of warm cinnamon bread and bit into it. "Bake as much as you like. I'll enjoy every bite." He closed his eyes and inhaled the spicy fragrance. "Mmmm. Albus is going to miss this, and I'm going to enjoy it. I'm glad we understand each other."

She smiled. She understood him. He hadn't understood her. Agreeing she heard him did not mean she agreed to stay silent. After all, if she could not share with her brother, why had God sent her here?

Later that afternoon, Syntyche stood in the middle of the empty house. Tymon's servants had carted everything away. All she needed to do was close the door and follow them home.

Her feet refused to move.

The house she and Alex had rented was no longer was hers, but it would belong to her forever, its memories sheltered in her heart.

Each crack in the wall was dear to her. The door that didn't latch well, the floor she'd swept ten thousand times, the loose stone in the hearth—each held a story, a giggle, a tear. The air still hummed with songs and Alex's deep laughter, still smelled of the spices she'd used in baking.

This part of her life, like one of the Hebrew scrolls, had been spooled and stored on a shelf. She could untie the fastening, unroll the dusty memories, but unlike the living Word of God, there was no one to share it with. No one to care how the cracks on the wall looked like a rabbit, or blush with her remembering the night when the faulty latch gave way in the wind.

Syntyche memorized the angle of each corner, the slight sag of the lowest shelf, the slant of uneven stones beneath her feet. Closing her eyes, she inhaled her home's own dusky scent one final time, drawing its taste, its sounds inward until she'd absorbed all of it into herself.

Only then did she make a final turn, walk through the door, and latch it—unsuccessfully—behind her. Starting down the street toward Tymon's home—her home—she looked forward, never glancing backward. This, she'd learned from Paul. Forgetting what lies behind, press forward toward what is ahead.

CHAPTER SIX

November

Euodia stood, arms held out straight from her sides, as Claudia dressed her for the day. When she folded and clipped the silk stola for the third time, Euodia noticed a tremor in the girl's hands. She lowered her arms, deterring her next attempt, and caught Claudia's wrist.

"You are troubled. Share with me what is wrong. Please."

Claudia pulled away and stared at the floor. "It will displease you."

Euodia added the slightest tinge of sternness to her voice. "I will be more displeased if you do not tell me."

The girl gnawed her lower lip before mumbling a reply. "Your mater-in-law and your husband have been talking."

Euodia laughed. "I hope so. She is his mater."

Claudia lifted her head enough that Euodia could see her eyes. "You will not like what they said about you, what they decided without considering you."

Euodia's heart began to pound. "Decided?" She searched the girl's face for any hint of cunning. Some of the staff resented that Marcellus's wife was not a noble like their master—just a merchant's daughter—and might not hesitate to cause trouble for her. "Wait. Claudia, is this a rumor or truth? Eventually, I will find out, and if it is untrue or hearsay, you will no longer work here."

"Truth. Ask Master Marcellus." Her gaze bored into Euodia's. "He has agreed his mater will host a feast for the Roman goddess, Juno."

Sweat prickled beneath her arms. "Where will the feast be held?"

"Here."

Aghast, Euodia stared at her servant.

"His mater said when you remembered the richness and gloriousness of Juno, you'd recover your senses and forget the shabby peasant you worship. Master Marcellus agreed to let her try and persuade you to return to Juno." Claudia shrugged. "Or Hera. I think they are the same. At least it is not March and time for the *Matronalia* with the races and burnt sacrifices. Invitations have already been sent and food ordered. This will not be too bad, just a feast."

A feast in honor of an idol, a block of stone, a creation made by a person no wiser or more powerful than herself. A feast that desecrated her beliefs and faith. A feast Marcellus knew she'd oppose. A feast he'd approved.

Disbelief blazed into betrayal. Horror exploded into fury—molten silver coursing through her veins. Head spinning, Euodia trembled uncontrollably. No words came. No thoughts formed—only emotion—clanging, galling, piercing her ten thousand times ten thousand.

Hands pushed her to sit, held her head as she vomited, wiped her mouth, pressed a cool cloth against her neck.

"Do you want me to call for Master Marcellus?"

Claudia's voice shrilled in her ear. Euodia pushed herself upright. Shook her head. If he walked in now, she'd scream vileness at him, hurl hurt she could never undo. If Mater Abigail appeared, she'd... Her fingers curled into claws.

"Leave." She flicked her hand for emphasis.

When the door clicked behind Claudia, Euodia sank to the floor. Bile surged again. She forced it down and pressed her face against the mosaic tile. The chill of the floor seeped through her skin, calming her, slowing her breathing. The throbbing in her head eased. The hurt did not.

She slept and woke to a wet nose nuzzling her ear. Linus. Scratching beneath his chin, she puzzled briefly. Remembered. She sat up and wrapped her arms around her knees. What to do?

Syntyche wouldn't flinch or hesitate. She'd march into Mater Abigail's room and confront her, flatly forbid her to invite friends into her home to honor Juno. She'd stand a handsbreadth away, feet apart, arms akimbo, and speak with such force no one would defy her.

She wasn't Syntyche.

Before Jesus became her Lord, the Euodia she'd been would have either hidden behind Syntyche or Tymon or Marcellus, or surrendered to avoid upsetting anyone. That wasn't her anymore.

"Lord, what do I do?"

Patience and kindness.

Ah. She remembered. "Love is patient, love is kind." It had been in Paul's first letter to the church in Corinth. It seemed sensible when Brother Clement first read it. But in this case? According to Claudia, the feast was a fact. Patience? Kindness to those desecrating her house? How did that fit in here? And love? Not what she was feeling toward Marcellus or his mater.

She straggled up from the floor, removed her rumpled stola and splashed water on her face and in her mouth. With a fresh under-tunic and warm stola from the clothes chest, she dressed herself, as she had for years before having her own servant. Unsure of the day's coolness, she shrugged into a wool palla. Looking neither left nor right, she left the house.

And walked. Back streets, side streets, with no heed to her directions, ignoring those who shouted for her to move to one side or those who stood in her way. The sun stared down from straight overhead before she paused and surveyed her surroundings. Ahead, a tall woman, elegantly dressed, stepped out of a shop and squinted in her direction.

"Euodia?"

"Lydia?" Mouth dry, her voice emerged as a whisper. "I thought you were out of town until April."

"Our Lord brought me home from Phoenicia earlier than I expected. Looking at your face, I know one reason. Come inside. You've been outside too long."

As her eyes adjusted from bright sun to indoor shadows, the room came alive—swaths of every purple imaginable draped the shelves—lavender and lilac, orchid and amethyst. Coiled magenta ribbons, plum-colored silks, and violet-hued pallas with lined hoods hung from hooks along the wall. Euodia thought back to when she'd been a child learning the color names. She'd never imagined so many shades of the simple word *purple*.

Lydia offered a cup of cool liquid. "No, it's not purple." She laughed. "Most everyone thinks it will be."

"Phoenicia? How interesting."

"Land of the finest purple dye. I have it shipped here as a solid. More expensive than the liquid but saves on paying for the weight of water. I can control the hues better also." Lydia tilted her head. "Our Lord did not direct your steps here to learn about purple dye, did He?"

Euodia dropped her mask of curiosity. "No." Agitated, she jiggled her foot. "I do not know what I should do—only what I want to do—scream."

"Fear?"

"Anger." She crossed her arms and scowled at a deep purple sash.

Lydia's eyebrows rose slightly. "My dyes do not fade no matter how harsh your glare."

"I'm sorry." Euodia pressed her hands against her eyes and clutched her head. "I cannot believe he agreed when he knew it was an affront to all I believe—or that he'd let his mater goad him into it." Releasing her head, she jerked her hands upward. "Does he care nothing about me?"

"'He' is your husband?"

"He and his mater determined to honor Juno at our house—a feast—with their town friends. They know I worship our Lord Jesus. They know this will upset me—infuriate me—and his mater does it intentionally."

"They are not believers in our Lord Jesus?"

"Of course they are not believers," Euodia snapped back.

Lydia pleated the nearest cloth. "Then, what did you expect?"

Silence weighted the room.

A mere arm's-length distance, a heartbeat away, Euodia heard the ebb and flow of life's busy pace. The rapid slap of children's sandals on marble slab roads, the squawking of the night's dinner, the rumble of carts and greetings of friends seasoned the outside air with ordinariness. Inside, time stilled. Mute, she sat without blinking.

Lydia pleated and smoothed, pleated and smoothed.

"Oh." Euodia's voice sounded as small as she felt. "Oh." She stared at her hands as though they were foreign objects. At last, she looked up. Lydia watched her. "What do I do? I understand now, but I'm still angry."

Kindness shone in Lydia's eyes. "Will you heed the words of a woman old enough to be your mater?"

"Gratefully."

"Dear girl, you are angry because your husband—what is his name?"

"Marcellus."

"Because Marcellus broke your trust. You believed he would think of your needs and wishes yet he chose to please his mater instead of you."

Euodia sniffled. "He chose her—and Juno."

"Your anger is a good sign."

At Euodia's disbelief, Lydia held up a hand to stop her protests. "It tells me you want to have a deep unity, a connection with him, and you are hurting because the unity is broken."

Euodia's chin wobbled. Tears spilled from her eyes. Impatiently, she brushed them away.

"If you scream at your Marcellus or scowl at his mater, you change nothing. The feast will be held. The friends will arrive. The goddess will be honored. You will break relationship with your husband and be viewed as contentious by your in-laws. Does this make you any different from them? Are you living out the grace of our Lord Jesus?"

Euodia huffed and crossed her arms. "So, I smile sweetly and say, 'What a lovely evening'?"

Lydia chuckled. "If you wish. I'd rather you ask the Lord to guide you in keeping your integrity while living out His love and compassion. Consider letting Him work through you to bring harmony rather than chaos."

"It feels as if I'm being unfaithful."

Lydia tapped her chin. "Paul told me a story about a God-fearing man, a commander of armies who was in a similar situation as you are. Let me think, what was his name? Naaman—that's it—who served a king, an idol worshiper. Naaman was commanded to escort the king into the idol's temple. The king leaned on him while bowing to the idol, which required Naaman to also bow as if he too worshiped the idol. Naaman trusted the Lord knew his heart was pure, so each time he entered the idol's temple, he asked our Lord to forgive him.

"Euodia, our God is a God of mercy and grace." She studied the younger woman's face. "Is it God you fear to displease or someone else?"

Euodia pinched her lips together and averted her gaze.

"I see. Another question, then. Are you angry Juno's feast will be held at your home or that Marcellus followed his mater's leading? You need not answer me, dear. It is between you and our Lord."

"It's wrong either way."

"Can our Lord bring good from it?"

Euodia grimaced. "I'm supposed to say 'yes,' but I don't see how He can."

"Child, this is called faith." Lydia chuckled. "We may not see the way, but we trust He does. We trust Him with what we do not understand, even what we do not like and especially what we fear."

Euodia put both hands over her mouth to hide the trembling of her chin. When she spoke, it was through the lattice of her fingers. "I'm angry but even more afraid—afraid Marcellus will never come to faith in our Lord. His parents disapprove of my faith. I think they fear he will desert the family gods." She leaned forward. "Lydia, if—"

As she shifted, a shaft of light struck her face. She glanced through the door at the sky, the sun's angle alerting her to the time. She'd been away from home most of the day with no explanation—another lapse in judgment Mater Abigail would notice.

"Lydia, I need to return home. I-I left unexpectedly this morning."

"I guessed as much. You wear no jewelry and carry no purse. Use my cisium. It's too cold to walk home—even for November." Lydia went to the back of the shop and called an order.

A few minutes later, nestled among the cart's deep purple cushions, Euodia pushed the hood of her palla to one side and poked her head out the open window. "Thank you, Lydia. You have given me a lot to consider during our time together. I'm thankful the Lord brought you home early."

Euodia welcomed the warmth of her house. Servants did not rush to greet her or lift the palla from her arms—a lapse in their duties but a respite she did not mind.

Her heart plummeted when Marcellus's servant approached before she reached the sanctuary of her room. She needed more time to calm her thoughts and decide how to speak with her husband. Her anger no longer boiled, but it simmered. She'd hoped it would have time to cool before they spoke.

"The master wishes to speak with you."

Knots tightening in her belly, she set her jaw and stiffened her shoulders. Unfastening her brooch and tossing the man her palla, she ignored the disapproval in his eyes. "I'll go to him immediately."

Lord?

There was no answer, no guidance.

Why had she asked? She didn't truly want to know.

Marcellus stood behind a chair, his eyes hooded as if he expected her fury to explode when she entered the room and he wanted to be as far from her as possible and with a table and chair between them.

Did her smile look as forced as it felt? Probably. His eyes narrowed more.

She sat and arranged the folds of her stola to cover her toes. Waiting for Marcellus to speak, she noticed his knuckles whiten as he clenched the back of the chair. He must wonder if she knew about Juno's feast or if he had to tell her. Spitefully, she let him wait.

"You left early and with no word to anyone."

"Yes."

"To take care of those Jesus people again?"

"No."

Uncomfortable silence deadened the room. She jiggled her foot, swishing the street-stained hem of her stola. He had summoned her here. He could start. She'd sit without speaking all evening before she apologized.

Refusing to look at him, she studied the painting closest to her chair—a fountain surrounded by flowers in full bloom with so many shades of…purple. Lydia's words echoed in her mind: *"Consider letting Him work through you…."*

Remorse stilled her foot, softened her carriage, eased the knot in her belly. Alienating Marcellus did nothing to honor her Lord Jesus.

Lord, this time I'm listening.

Humility.

Exactly what she didn't want to hear. She'd asked, though, and chose to obey.

"I'm sorry to have worried you, Marcellus. It was wrong of me. I'll apologize to your mater."

The tightness around his eyes eased.

"I understand invitations to attend a feast honoring Juno have been sent to many of your parents' friends and probably to some of our friends. I'm told it will be held here, in our home."

His eyes flickered, acknowledging it was true.

Speaking with caution, she navigated each word—mossy stepping stones across storm-filled rapids—and dared approach Juno's feast.

"Marcellus." Hesitating, she added "Beloved" and found she meant it.

Lord?

Unity.

"You honor your parents and their beliefs. You are a loving and unselfish son. If we are ever blessed with a son, I hope he will be like you."

Infinitesimally, Marcellus pulled back. Disbelief darkened his eyes.

Voice soft, hands relaxed in her lap, she chose gentle words. "I wish this had not been asked of you. I wish it was not in our home. I wish it did not honor something I cannot accept." She smiled. "But it was asked. It will be in our home. I accept your decision."

Marcellus's gaze bore into hers as if probing for a glint of sarcasm or falsehood. "My pater requires you to attend." His aggressive tone dared her to defy him.

A groan escaped. She clenched her jaw, biting her tongue, willing her lips to remain closed.

Lord! Help! This is too much! It cannot be pleasing to You.

Unity.

Euodia drew in a long breath and released it slowly. Clasping her hands, she smiled to loosen her jaw. "I will honor your pater's wish."

His look of bewilderment almost made her laugh.

"Marcellus, I cannot and will not honor Juno, not to please you nor your parents nor Caesar. To me, she is a lump of rock a talented sculptor chiseled into the form of a woman. You know I believe in the one and only living God. He alone will I worship."

He eyed her without speaking, but his hands no longer gripped the back of his chair.

"I refuse to honor a rock, but I will honor you as my husband."

Atticus strode into the room. "Marcellus, did you speak firmly to your wife? She knows she must comply with my demand? No excuses will be tolerated. No whining petulance permitted."

Before Marcellus responded, Euodia stood and smiled at her pater-in-law. "Marcellus shared your order. I will do as you wish, Pater." With a dip of her head, she swept from the room. His words followed her out the door.

"Well done, Marcellus. She knows her master and obeys."

Euodia smothered a laugh. She did know her Master, but it was not who Atticus thought it was.

CHAPTER SEVEN

December

Syntyche bustled through the front door of Clement's home, her arms filled with baskets bulging with bread and pastries still warm from her oven.

"Helena, greetings! Look, I brought extra bread to give the widows and sick. When I moved in with my brother, he said to bake as much as I wished. So, I did." She winked. "I think he meant for him, but he didn't specify. It's one good thing that's come of me losing my job and returning home—a constantly full larder." She looked around. "Is Euodia here? She can help carry some of this. She always wishes we had more to give away."

"No. She's not." Helena twisted her hands. "Have you spoken to her recently?"

Syntyche lowered the baskets to the floor. "No, why?" She pressed a hand against her lower back and stretched. "Bread is heavier than you'd imagine. What else do we have to share?"

"Fruit, fish, soap. Last time I spoke with Euodia—it's been several months—she was upset."

"She upsets herself often. Don't worry about her. She'll be fine." She patted the older woman's shoulder and peered past her. "Will Brother Clement be coming with us today?"

"This might be different." Helena fidgeted with her sleeve. "She was teary-eyed over something I said and has been avoiding me at church."

"No, Euodia adores you—thinks of you as the mater we lost." Syntyche paused and looked at her sharply. "Helena, what did you say that was so distressing?"

Helena suddenly seemed very interested in the floor. "I chided her for her ungracious behavior when Cerberus thanked you for leading him to faith. I fear it will be remembered more than Cerberus's testimony. Others have commented on it."

"They did?" She shrugged. "I've heard nothing about it except from Malitta."

"Malitta is joining you today instead of Clement."

Disappointment washed through Syntyche. Sharing day was one of the rare times she had to speak with him alone, one of the few times he seemed to see her as Syntyche instead of a member of the church.

"Your sister is resentful and bitter, so I counseled her to apologize to you. Tension between believers can poison a church, distract from God's message. You must forgive her, Syntyche. She's your sister in the Lord as well as…"

Syntyche's hand brushed the air in dismissal. "Helena, I could never stay angry with Euodia."

Trudging to Clement's after the long day, Euodia called herself a coward for continuing to avoid Helena by lingering outside the house until her sister and Malitta emerged. Nevertheless, as they headed back, she knew she'd decline the offer to stop and share the details of their day with the excuse there was one more visit she planned—to sweep the floors of a woman who'd injured her shoulder.

She'd already tuned out Syntyche's admonitions that she and Malitta must season their ministries with teachings of the Lord—liberally adding Him into their conversations as if they were making a spicy relish with an abundance of chili peppers. Her sore feet and growling stomach spoke louder than anyone's words.

She was not bold and brave like her sister. Frowns, shrugs, sneers—nothing daunted Syntyche. Rebuffs bounced her to the next person. Indifference bolstered her spirits. Debates delighted her.

A whiff of rosemary carried her to the day's first visit and the gratitude of a chairbound youth. Washing the girl's lice-speckled hair with chrysanthemum powder killed the insects. Rinsing it in rosemary tincture then combing the short strands until they dried brought sighs of pleasure to the thin young face. Before leaving, she'd whispered one little message in the girl's ear. "Jesus cares for you."

Maybe she'd not said enough.

Skidding wheels and the restless prance of halted hooves jolted her thoughts to the present.

"Euodia?"

A familiar face peered through the window of an ornately embellished *carpentum*. Euodia glimpsed portraits of Roman goddesses painted on the ceiling and walls.

"Valeria!"

The horse closest to her bared its teeth. She stepped back, shading her face as its gleaming silver bridle threw sun in her eyes.

Valeria gestured her closer. "Why are you walking in the streets? Did a wheel break on your carpentum? You look as if you've fallen. Were you hurt? Where are your servants? Why didn't you summon a covered litter? Euodia, come ride with me. There's plenty of room. Let's get you home." Her nose wrinkled. "Your clothes, your hair—by all the gods in Rome, what happened to you?"

Before she could protest, Valeria pushed aside the curtains, releasing a gush of flowery perfume. Euodia felt her face burn at her soiled clothing and limp hair. Dirt stained her fingernails, and the odor of the day's work filmed her skin. She resisted scratching her head. Had lice transferred their affections from the girl to her?

"You are so kind, my friend, but I prefer to walk."

A flash of relief sparked in Valeria's eyes before being disguised with a shake of her head. "As you wish. We will have time to visit at Juno's feast. I'm delighted you and Marcellus are hosting it this year. How did you ever coax him to agree? Next week, yes? I've heard this feast will be the year's entertainment not to miss. For you, Euodia, I'll break my rule and arrive almost on time."

Wiggling her fingers in a quick wave, Valeria closed the carriage door.

Relieved, Euodia jumped backward, saving her toes from the wheels. She imagined Valeria's shock if she'd answered her barrage of questions.

"*What?*"

She spun to face Syntyche and Malitta's shock.

Stunned, Syntyche stared at her sister. Unable to speak, she shook her head—a futile attempt to comprehend the incomprehensible.

She shivered. The ringing in her ears deepened to a deafening roar as if the powerful northwest *vardar* blew down the mountains. Lightheaded, mouth dry, she forced deep breaths into her lungs and tried to swallow.

That woman had mistaken Euodia for someone else. Syntyche's heart sank. No, Valeria called Euodia by name—several times—and referred to Marcellus. Then surely she'd imagined the woman's words—or tired and hungry, she'd misunderstood the words said. Words she'd never have believed unless she'd heard them herself.

But she had heard them.

A curtain of guilt shrouded Euodia's face. She denied nothing. Explained nothing. Apologized for nothing.

"You… I…" Thoughts refused to form. Her gaze probed Euodia's eyes searching for answers or understanding or a glimmer of remorse.

Disbelief eased into belief.

Denial gave way to dismay.

Euodia had forsaken the Lord.

Fear and grief unleashed anger.

"You faithless hypocrite."

Euodia's face blanched.

"I am ashamed to call you sister."

Her sister flinched like she'd done as a child when someone's ire turned on her. Syntyche had never imagined she'd be the one Euodia shrank from. It did not stop her from continuing.

"You have betrayed our Lord. How dare you call yourself a Christ follower when you host a feast to Juno in your own home?"

Syntyche shook off Malitta's restraining hand.

"You have destroyed your witness." Syntyche stomped away, pivoted, and returned.

"Your good works are nothing but deceit. My love for you has blinded me to who you truly are. More fool me. You—you traitor. Have you no shame? Nothing to say for yourself?"

Euodia's violent trembling stilled Syntyche's words.

Malitta pushed between the sisters to wrap an arm around Euodia. "Take this out of the people's watch, Syntyche. They are staring at us, and some of them I recognize from your church. Maybe we should take her to her house."

"I'll never enter her house again—it's become a temple to Juno."

Malitta frowned. "You are too harsh with her."

"Then we will take her to Clement's. He can deal with her flagrant dishonor of the Lord."

"I thought Christ followers were merciful." Malitta glared at Syntyche. "Not sure I want more of this Christ."

Resolute, Syntyche stalked toward Clement's house. If Clement and Helena couldn't dissuade Euodia, she'd argue, beg, or cajole—whatever it took to free her beloved little sister from Juno's stony grip. Gradually, her pace slowed. Drained from her outburst, the day's exertion, and raw grief, she felt her ire cooling, congealing into a thick clump. Her feet dragged, each step requiring more effort.

The strain and disappointment of the last month crept through her shoulders, pressing them into a curve. A lump tightened her throat.

She felt old. Tired. Somehow she'd failed her little sister—and, she suspected, failed her Lord and Malitta.

In a stupor, Euodia allowed Malitta to propel her through the streets to Clement's house, although she wanted to wrest loose and flee to the safety of her room and the comfort of Linus's wiggly acceptance. She'd expected Syntyche's fierce reaction, but its viciousness, the violent rock-hard words slung to bruise and break her, had been unexpected.

Struggling to remain upright—not drop to the street and curl into a ball like a pill bug—she tried to ignore Malitta's questions, but the words—and reproach—penetrated. "We're almost there. Can you walk any faster? My feet hurt. What do you think Clement will say? I admit I'm surprised at you—well, Syntyche too. Aren't you leaders among the women? Can you worship both Juno and Jesus?"

More than ever, Euodia wanted to be a pill bug. Despite divine nudging to confide in her sister, she'd ignored opportunities to explain her acceptance of the feast and the Lord's leading. Of course, Syntyche did not understand. Resentment flickered. She could have asked instead of assuming Euodia had abandoned her Savior. Did her sister understand her so little that she'd discard years of confidences and trustworthiness from one overheard conversation?

Why had the Lord allowed Valeria to drive through the streets at a time she should have been home resting for whatever evening festivities the popular matron been invited to attend? Why did Valeria announce the feast to everyone in earshot?

Euodia snorted. That one she knew the answer to. Valeria basked in having all eyes and ears attuned to Valeria. Today, her flawless complexion and hair, the rich purple of her silk stola denoting her nobility, and riding in the city's finest carpentum had not been enough. She'd needed to be heard as well as seen. Poor woman, if she only knew the One who saw and heard her—loved her when no one else did. *Lord, how do I tell her?*

Show her.

Malitta elbowed her. "Stop smiling. We're here. Clement will believe you have no remorse."

Euodia welcomed the quietness of the house if not the upcoming interrogation. She rubbed her arm when Malitta released her grip as though she'd delivered a prisoner and was no longer responsible. Syntyche sent the servant who'd opened the door to request Clement's presence.

Her heart sank when Helena appeared. Helena already assumed the worst of her.

Quelling the urge to turn and escape, Euodia followed the others as Helena led them to Clement's office.

"My son will be here in a moment. I'll send for refreshments."

Helena gave the order then hovered near the door, evidently curious about the visit. Clement arrived, and she followed him inside.

Euodia lowered her eyes as he surveyed their bedraggled appearance, knowing he'd not miss the tension in their faces, the set of their shoulders, the crossed arms. Tears pooled when he spoke.

"Syntyche?"

Euodia's hopes of being heard plummeted at that one word. She'd long ago recognized—though Syntyche had not—Clement's interest in her vivacious sister.

Syntyche and Malitta first recounted the day's events—excluding her lice cleaning—then repeated every word of the encounter with Valeria. Euodia fastened her gaze on a purple flower in the mosaic.

Lord?

Patience.

She'd rather have heard "retribution" or "vengeance is Mine" or even "apology coming," but she'd learned after almost six years of faith that the Lord seldom spoke the words she wanted Him to say—even when she offered hints.

Syntyche and even Malitta fell silent. She sensed Clement watching her, felt waves of shock emanating from Helena.

Lord?

Patience.

Her knees wobbled as fatigue threatened to overwhelm her. If she could lie down and sleep, maybe she'd awaken to discover this was a bad dream. At least she'd be able to think how to explain. How to forgive the humiliation of being shamed on a public street then dragged before a church leader.

Patience.

Yes, Lord.

She looked up. Clement's head was bowed in prayer. Helena stared at her with distaste. Malitta stood, lips pursed, arms crossed. The servants carrying refreshment, their eyes bulging, waited by the door. Syntyche swiped at a tear.

Gratitude flooded her. Syntyche still cared, and Clement prayed. Yes, the servants would whisper, but Helena would hear the truth. Malitta would…continue to confound her.

Clement raised his head. Eyes riveted on hers, he motioned for her to speak. "Euodia?"

Words did not come. She cleared her throat. Tried again. A voice she did not recognize as her own croaked. No drink was offered. She refused to ask. Swallowed until a servant hurried forward with a chalice of water.

She smiled into the concerned eyes of the servant and silently gave thanks for the tender mercy.

"Last week, my in-laws arrived.…" She kept her story short, omitting little, confessing her anger with Marcellus, her defiance to the Lord, and Lydia's wise guidance.

Glancing around the room, she saw skepticism, understanding, and dismay.

"Syntyche, I wronged you by not confiding to you what had happened. You would never allow your home to be overtaken or your life determined for you, and I feared your disapproval. You are stronger than I am—"

Clement interrupted. "There are different strengths, Euodia. Your strength is in listening to the Lord. We need to imitate that strength of yours."

From the corner of her eye, Euodia saw her sister bristle.

Helena tapped her son's arm. "You approve of Euodia's actions? I don't."

He stroked the length of his beard. "Mater, would you have her alienate her husband and his family by being defiant? Would that open their heart and minds to our Lord?"

"But to host a feast to a pagan goddess?" Helena twisted her fingers in the folds of her stola.

"I wish Brother Syzygus were here to advise me." Clement exhaled long and deeply. "From my place on earth as a mere mortal, it seems wrong to me too, Mater, but she sought the Lord's guidance, and this is how He directed her—first to Lydia, then in her responses to Marcellus and his pater. It is not to our understanding. What good our Lord will bring from this honor for Juno, I cannot imagine, but I wait with great hope, and with great wonder and joy of being part of His plan."

Euodia slumped as the tension drained, leaving her even more exhausted. Tears prickled her eyes. "Brother Clement, later may we talk further about how I should manage this? Word will spread and cause dissension among the believers."

He nodded and started to speak, but she interrupted him. "Please, I must return home immediately."

"Of course." His eyes twinkled. "I can't offer you a horse-drawn carpentum, but we have a mule and cart." His gaze shifted to Syntyche. "Sister, stay if you can. I need to talk with you."

Malitta stepped forward and grasped her arm. "My home is the same direction. I'll see she arrives safely."

Neither Helena nor Syntyche bade them farewell.

Syntyche crossed her arms and breathed deeply to steady herself while she waited for Clement's return from seeing Syntyche and Malitta into the cart. She'd never before been reprimanded by another church leader, much less Clement. After this, his occasional glimmer of interest in her, his lingering glances would cease. He'd think of her as a church problem, not as a woman.

Embarrassment turned to irritation. He had no right to chastise her. He hadn't been there—hadn't been shocked and grieved—everything she believed about someone distorted beyond recognition. If he'd heard those words about his mater, he'd have spoken as sternly as she had instead of calmly requesting an explanation or suggesting they take a stroll and chat privately.

Nor would Paul have stood calmly by if he'd witnessed what she had. He'd approve of her directness and censure Euodia for her timidity. He'd written to the church in Galatia and called them foolish. He'd not be squeamish about her confronting her own sister.

She tapped her fingers against her arm, its staccato keeping pace with her rising ire. How dare Clement embarrass her by telling her to stay when the others left. Maybe he should not be the church leader if he acted this way. He may as well have announced to everyone he did not support her standing up for the Lord. No, he was going to reprove her. It was cruel. Unkind. Unnecessary. UnChristlike.

She'd never do anything like— She gulped.

Clement returned. She followed his leather-clad feet as they crossed the room and stopped in front of her. White lines marked where sandal straps prevented the sun's browning.

"Sister Syntyche, I pray you and Euodia will reconcile, but what happened today is between you and the Lord unless you feel led to talk with me or Brother Syzygus about it." He paused as if waiting for her to decide then stepped away and sat down. "I asked you to stay to talk with you about resuming your baking and cooking ministry to the women. Are you willing to pray about doing this?"

Bewildered, she gaped up at him. This is why he told her to remain behind? She nodded. Spluttered a yes.

"It would be better if the lessons and teaching of Jesus occurred at your brother's house instead of here. Since I am an unmarried man, some of the community might hesitate to come to my house even though Mater lives here with me—and of course, there can be no hint of scandal. I understand your brother's house has a large kitchen too."

Tymon's words sped through her mind. *"Do not bring those Jews or Jesus people or anyone else here."* But these women were not believers or Jews—most were Greek—just people who wanted to become better cooks and bakers. That's why they came, not to hear of Jesus—although they did as often as she could manage to mention His name. What harm could it do?

"Brother Clement." Voice breathy, her heart pounding in relief, she pressed a hand against her chest. Maybe he'd think she was honored he'd asked. "Give me a week to sort it out with Tymon, and then we'll let it be known the lessons are available."

"And Euodia?"

Syntyche's gaze veered to one side. "We're sisters. She knows I love her."

Clement frowned.

"She understands I only want what's best for her and spoke out of concern. But if you wish, I'll talk to her."

CHAPTER EIGHT

January AD 61

Euodia wiggled her toes into the luxurious pile of the rug Amelia had brought with her from the villa. It was thicker and heavier than any floor covering she'd ever stepped on. She pitied the menservants who rolled it, carried it, and arranged it every time Amelia visited. Then again, the men might have it easier than Amelia's female servants, who must watch her every second to not miss a subtle command.

Euodia shifted in her chair, trying to hide her restlessness. When she'd agreed to the banquet in Juno's honor, she'd believed that was all required of her. Never had she expected her attendance—though not opinion or approval—was required for much of the planning.

She squirmed. Here she sat, doing nothing while a new believer grieved the death of her dearest friend, and another needed help because she'd broken her leg, and someone else was being evicted from his home. So many called on her for help or comfort, and she longed to go to them.

Euodia knew the tip of her tongue would fall off if she had to bite it much more. Holding her breath to prevent critical words spewing from her mouth worked, but she grew lightheaded. Distracting herself by counting floor tiles or how many times Amelia talked about herself made her sleepy.

If she didn't do something, she'd cause trouble she didn't want to face. She eyed the parchment littering the floor. The one time she'd stooped to pick up and straighten a pile, Amelia barked a command to stop interfering.

Plans for her wedding and the feast following it had not caused this much commotion. She cringed to think all this expense and time and effort was being invested in a meal for a rock with a face.

Her foot swished back and forth, earning a frown of disapproval from Amelia. She wanted to frown back. Amelia's plans for the feast were made with muted murmurings between herself and two of her servants. Vendors' wares had been strewn across the floor awaiting purchase or dismissal.

Lord, how much longer?

Patience.

Euodia squirmed. She'd practiced patience enough today. Why did the Lord give her such answers, knowing she'd dislike obeying them?

Marcellus entered the room and seemed surprised to find her there.

"You are helping plan the festivities? I did not expect so much of you, Euodia. Are you at ease doing this?"

She hoped her face displayed a smile and not a grimace. "I'm only keeping your mater company."

He glanced around the room then held out his hand to her. "Mater, I require my wife's presence. She will be unavailable to you for the remainder of the day."

Grasping his hand, Euodia almost skipped out of the room. Out of sight and hearing, she flung her arms around him. "You rescued me!"

"You must pay the price." He tugged her toward the front of the house where one square room was dedicated to his art. "I've something to show you."

Euodia allowed herself a small skip. Rarely was she invited into his art studio. Marcellus whisked away the cloth concealing his work.

Mesmerized, she studied the painting. The young nymph, clad in a gossamer stola, plucked wildflowers of blue and purple to match the crown nestled atop her dark tresses. To one side a river flowed, from the other side grew a forest thick with undergrowth from which two tiny eyes peered.

"How do you do this, Marcellus? I can almost hear her speaking. And the woodland creature—it will venture forward any second."

"You like it?"

"Immensely."

"I thought to have it frescoed on your bedroom wall."

Between squeals of delight, Marcellus received another hug.

"Hush, Wife. Pater will hear you and banish you to Mater's room again."

She quieted and returned to study the painting from different angles.

"Euodia, why do you sit attendance on Mater? You realize she's planning Juno's feast?"

She circled to face him. "For unity. For you. For us." She leaned her head against his chest. "I asked my Lord, and He showed me I must not be the cause of dissension in our home."

Marcellus held her close. She wished she could see his face and know his thoughts.

Euodia stared in dismay as another delivery arrived from her in-laws' villa. Already her home appeared to have been confiscated, her carefully chosen and curated furniture systematically shifted to a back storage area and replaced with Amelia's ornate furnishings. The dining area had not been touched, but who knew what these boxes concealed.

"Mistress, that housekeeper you hired quit. Where do you want these crates and pallets placed?"

Old Felix looked ready to cry. He liked routine and order, not chaos. Everything had become chaotic. There was no more room in the cluttered living space or in storage. Euodia rubbed her temples where a headache began to form.

"Mistress." The kitchen boy who helped with Linus shifted from foot to foot. "Cook refuses to step outside her room. She wants to talk with you. I think she's going to quit."

Why did no one listen to her? She'd warned her, but Cook, having capitulated and allowed others in to her sacred space, had lost control of her kitchen. For the last week, she'd refused to even enter the cooking area, much less prepare meals.

"Mistress, do we have to obey Lady Amelia's servants?" Claudia must have taken pitiful-puppy-eyes lessons from Linus.

Felix's wife was not pitiful. She was angry. "Mistress, nothing is being ordered for the kitchen except fancy things we can't eat. Mistress, who eats jellyfish? That man says his food is for the feast, but we're hungry."

"Mistress—"

Euodia held up a hand to stop the clamor. "Felix, I have no idea what to tell you. Ask Atticus. They are his belongings, he will need to decide.

"Child, tell Cook I will see her soon. Find Linus and take him with you to amuse her until I arrive."

Felix shuffled off in search of Atticus as the kitchen boy raced to find Linus.

"Claudia, only Linus's puppy eyes work with me. You follow my orders, but you treat the others with respect."

Euodia motioned to Felix's wife. "Come with me. We will make a list of what you believe is needed. Can you order it?"

The woman's quick nod assured her she knew what needed to be done. Euodia beckoned the last plaintiff closer. "What is your concern?"

"Lady Amelia requires your presence."

Euodia shook her head. "I cannot attend to her right now. Tell her I'll be there after I've spoken to my cook and made a list of needed supplies with my servant."

Fear shriveled the girl's face. "Please, mistress, Lady Amelia expects you to come with me now. She'll be very angry."

"Lady Amelia will understand and graciously wait if she wants dinner tonight."

Tears filled the young eyes. "Please?"

Sympathizing, Euodia lifted the girl's quivering chin. "Tell her I am appalled." She winked. "No, you must gloat and say I am distraught and horrified to learn food has not been restocked and I dare not face her if I can only provide servants' fare for her meals. She'll be so pleased at my failure, she'll not think to punish you when I don't come immediately."

Gratitude sparkled in the girl's wet eyes.

"Dry your eyes and run back faster than a little rabbit. Let's not keep her waiting."

If only it was so easy to solve all the problems. In one week, the banquet would be held. How much longer would her in-laws stay in town? Long enough to receive the adulations of their guests and praise from the priests who tended Juno's temple. Afterward, all the furniture and decorations must be repacked and shipped back to the villa. Another six weeks?

Lord, how much longer?

"Mistress."

It was not the voice of the Lord. Weary, she turned to face the next demand.

Compassion filled the servant's voice. "This will not go on forever."

Or maybe it was the voice of the Lord.

Euodia blinked and reached for a wall to steady herself. Had she worked too hard this morning helping a new family move into their house, becoming so tired she'd wandered into someone else's home instead of her own?

Unfamiliar sculptures lined the walls obscuring the garden wall paintings she and Marcellus commissioned when they first moved into the house. Busts of the family ancestors proclaiming their noble lineage, and of Atticus and Amelia and Marcellus—none of her, she noted—stood at intervals throughout the room.

The broad, intricately carved wooden couches that she'd ordered for this room had been replaced with ivory versions she recognized from her in-laws' estate. Six couches crowded the room instead of its usual three, each forming a U shape so eighteen people could be seated instead of the usual nine. Amelia's silver vessels of every size and shape shone on the ivory table in the middle of each set. Each place setting held a cup, plate, bowl, and spoon—all silver, all gleaming in the light from the candles and braziers.

"Mistress."

Euodia angled her head toward the voice. "It's so different. I had no idea all this had been changed or that there would be so many guests."

"Come along now. No more time to spend admiring the changes."

She bristled at the audacity of Amelia's servant speaking to her as if to a child.

"Maybe my mistress will leave them here for you when she returns to our estate."

Euodia hoped she wouldn't.

"Guests will begin arriving soon. Lady Amelia is having her hair dressed with scented ointments and requires yours to also be dressed with scents. She chose scents for you."

Well, that was terrible news. She wrinkled her nose. Scented fat rubbed into her thick straight hair rendered it a stringy mess of black rat tails instead of the silky clean tresses Marcellus called strands of midnight.

She followed the servant to where Amelia lounged as servants prepared her hair and nails for the festivities. A rainbow of clothes covered the bed while her mater-in-law debated the merits and flaws of each garment before choosing one for the evening.

"Mater Amelia, you will be the most stylish of anyone here tonight."

They both knew she spoke truth. Amelia accepted her due with a graceful nod. "Sit there. My hairdresser will scent your hair."

"No."

Pushed once again against her will, the seed of defiance broke through years of silent compliance to become a tender sprout.

"Mater Amelia, of course I would honor your wishes if at all possible, but Marcellus dislikes my hair oiled and scented. I know you'd not want me to disregard my husband's preferences."

Amelia never allowed a frown to mar her smooth skin. Her expressive eyes and voice, however, were well-honed weapons she handled with impressive skill.

Daggers flew from her eyes though she voiced the only acceptable answer. "Juno has given you wisdom. You must please my son above all others, including myself."

Left unsaid—"Even your God."

Valeria's flamboyant entrance occurred—as promised—almost on time. Trailing behind her paraded the brood of young matrons she ruled with her lifted eyebrow, nod, or turned shoulder. Euodia watched her finger the emeralds at her neck as she scrutinized the profusion of flowers and candles, statues and silver. Her lips curved upward in appreciation. For once, Valeria's approval brought no pleasure.

To hide her newfound indifference to Valeria's opinion, Euodia welcomed each woman with a kiss on the cheek and exclaimed over something for each one—a pearl crusted pendant, a hairstyle, a flattering color.

"You are welcome in my home. Allow my servant to show you to your places."

Just outside the incense-clouded room, musicians played songs of Juno's glory on lyres and flutes. Euodia watched the women as they were led past the guards and musicians into the dining area. At their whispers and giggles, she guessed they'd noticed the carefully selected and well-groomed male waiters filling silver cups with wine—cups decorated with images of Juno.

Arrangements of lilies and roses, the flowers associated with Juno, filled the room with their scent.

Dismayed, she slipped into another room to calm herself. Everything about this feast seemed wrong—was wrong—her presence an illusion of consent. Hot tears welled. Had she misunderstood the Lord's direction?

"Euodia."

Marcellus's voice startled her.

"My dear, I've been looking for you, to speak privately. I hesitate to tell you this before the feast. It is upsetting, but you need to know in case it surfaces during the banquet. Pater will be livid if you do not attend tonight. Are you strong enough to hear this now?"

Now, that she hardly breathed with fear? She nodded.

"A messenger arrived from your friend Helena. It is disturbing news and late arriving. Your brother assumes she is with you, and her friends believe her to be with her brother. I'm not sure how the truth was discovered, but I hope I intercepted the message before it reached the ears of Pater's guards."

She, who? Fingers curled into her clothes, her mind raced to make sense of Marcellus's words. Helena? Was she hurt? And the two of them not at peace? Or Clement and Syzygus—dead? Who? No. Paul—killed!

"Seven days ago, your sister—"

She covered her heart to still its thumping. "Synee's hurt? Dead?"

Marcellus grimaced. "Worse. Imprisoned."

"*What?*"

"Woman! Lower your voice. Do you want all of Philippi to know of this disgrace?"

Her hands flew to her mouth. She spoke through her fingers. "Why? What has she done?"

"She's accused of being a nuisance in proclaiming her God." Marcellus rubbed the back of his neck. "Euodia, will you keep this quiet until our guests leave? Will you do this for me? Pater and Mater will be angry enough when they learn of it, without having their feast ruined with whispered dialogue about your sister and thus, you."

Humility.

She'd neither asked for the Lord's direction nor wanted it. She wanted to race to the prison and free her sister, not smile and sit attendance at a feast she disapproved of wholeheartedly. She'd obeyed Him before, and it resulted in harsh words from her sister and this terrible evening. This was living for the Lord?

Struggling between obedience to the Lord or rushing to her sister's rescue, she turned her back.

"I need to find a way to have her released. An official order, a bribe…something."

"Euodia, I'm asking you to wait until after the banquet, not demanding it of you."

She winced. Shame heated her face. Marcellus showed humility while she balked at following the Lord's direction. Why did she fight obedience to her Savior? Would she ever simply reply, "Yes, Lord" without fighting Him? Maybe. Maybe not, but today she could obey.

She turned to face Marcellus. "Yes. I will do this for you."

He caught her hand and pulled her toward him. "Thank you. We have much to discuss but not now. Pater is waiting."

Hands clasped, they entered the dining area as the dancing girls exited and servants carrying doves scurried to their assigned places. In each corner stood a basin of perfumed water. One by one, a dove was submerged in the water then released to fly about the room scattering perfumed droplets on the guests.

Cooks presented their creations of stuffed wild boar, re-feathered pheasants, and platters of shellfish arranged in Juno's image. Stomach in knots, Euodia accepted food on her plate and pushed it into small mounds before flattening them, so it looked as if she'd eaten. If Mater Amelia believed she sulked and did not participate, this attempt at unity would fail.

She turned her head, pretending to watch the guests, the new group of dancers, the circling doves, but her mind filled with images of Syntyche shivering in a dank prison. A hovering waiter refilled her cup. She lifted it, set it down untouched. Syntyche suffered thirst. So would she. Weary, she sat upright. Syntyche would not sleep for fear of hungry rodents. Mater glared at her. She did not wilt. A harsh look did not compare to the danger Synee faced from other prisoners.

She knew the minute news of her sister's arrest filtered into her home. A slave sped across the room to Valeria and without pausing to ask permission, whispered in her ear. Valeria's eyes widened. She glanced at Euodia. Scorn flashed across her face before she turned to the person beside her, whispered, and another set of eyes widened, glanced at Euodia then turned to the one beside her.

Lord?

Patience.

More eyes shifted their gaze to her. Soon, Atticus and Amelia would notice and discover why their daughter-in-law was the focus of so many guests who'd gathered to honor Juno.

Atticus's eyes narrowed. An imperceptible signal summoned a guard who bent low to speak to his commander. Euodia kept her face serene even as her heart sank. If the guard knew, Marcellus had not intercepted Helena's message in time.

Abruptly, Atticus stood. Clapped his hands. The dancers fled. Musicians stilled their instruments. Waiters and cooks stepped backward.

"We are here today to honor the great goddess, Juno."

He quieted the cheering with an upheld hand. "I have prepared a gift for the joy of my life, my only son, my beloved son, and his wife."

Euodia noticed he worded it so as not to call her "beloved."

Four men rolled a large, shrouded object into the room.

Atticus strode forward. With a flourish he released the cloth covering a statue of Juno. "I present to this house, a gift. It is to honor my dear son, whose art has been commissioned in Rome, and in remembrance of tonight's feast. All glory and praise to Juno, the queen, the goddess of marriage."

Was all quiet or did the room ring with cheers? Euodia's heart pounded so loudly she heard nothing else but the throbbing in her ears. Marcellus tugged at her hand. She stood, followed him to stand before Atticus. Lydia had said to ask the Lord to help her keep her integrity. Frantic, she whispered a prayer.

Marcellus's mouth moved. Atticus nodded and clapped him on the shoulder then turned to her.

His voice came from far away. "Euodia?"

Euodia approached the statue. Circled it. Touched the cool marble hands, the painstakingly chiseled curls surrounding the smooth stone face, the delicate folds of the statue's garment.

"Pater Atticus, I've never seen such beautiful marble or such exquisite craftsmanship. You are a generous man."

The approval in his eyes meant nothing to her. The surrounding peace meant everything. She had remained humble, spoken truth, and not honored Juno. *Thank You, Lord.*

Night faded before all the guests had stumbled out the door to their carriages and drivers waiting with stoic horses. Valeria and her entourage had swept past without a word. Some had peered down at her as if she were the one arrested. Two guests had thanked her for the evening as if unaware of her sister's disgrace. When Atticus and Amelia bade the last guest goodbye and retired for the evening, Euodia gathered the yawning servants.

"You worked hard this evening. Leave the cleaning until morning. Go to your beds."

"But Lady Amelia—"

Euodia waved her hand in dismissal. "…is not the mistress of this house. I am. I will be obeyed by all of you. Complain to her tomorrow after you are rested."

Amid grateful smiles and murmured thanks, they scattered, and Euodia sought her own room, thinking only of stretching out to sleep. Marcellus stood between her and her bed.

She was surprised when her husband smiled. "No, Euodia. I'm tired too. Tomorrow, walk with me where we cannot be overheard. There are things I want to speak of that for now must remain only between us."

He guided her across the room, pushed her to sit on the bed, and knelt. As he removed her house sandals, she kissed the top of his head.

He raised his head and met her lips. "You did well tonight, Wife. Now sleep. Tomorrow we will talk."

The door clicked. Paw covering his face, Linus did not budge from the place he claimed near the foot of the bed. She tucked her feet against his warm tummy and curled into a ball. She did not stir until morning.

CHAPTER NINE

Syntyche shivered and scooted away from the damp stone walls. Maybe the middle of her cell would be warmer. It was not—the scum on the stone floor was dank and cold as the walls.

"I am honored to suffer for my Lord as Paul and Timothy and Silas did in this very place." She sneezed. "Deeply honored." She wiped her dripping nose on the hem of her skirt. "But I think they had warmer clothes than I do."

It hadn't felt an honor to have her arms grabbed, to be yanked along uneven ground, dragged up stone steps, and thrust into a cell. Peering through the darkness, she sighed. Alone. No one to talk to.

"Lord, if there's no one here to tell about You, why am I here? Is it to grow my faith?"

She drew her legs to her chest and wrapped her arms around them, seeking comfort and warmth. How had Paul endured this misery after being flogged?

Rejoice.

"I did, Lord! I said I was honored to suffer for You, and I am, but I'm also cold and thirsty and tired." She scratched the bites on her face.

As she rested her head on her knees, images of Euodia's face entered her mind. Her sweet little sister could not have borne this.

"Thank You, Lord, that by Your grace she is not here with me."

Not that she would ever be in this situation. Euodia did not endanger herself for the sake of sharing the Good News.

She froze at a scurry of tiny claws. Too close. She drew herself in tighter.

"You are a God of mercy to allow neither she nor Tymon to witness my arrest."

Tymon would be furious when he found out she'd been imprisoned. She understood it was an honor. Others would perceive it as disgraceful. If Tymon turned her out of the house, would Helena and Clement take her in?

Fur touched her ankles. "No!" She jerked them away and tucked them closer to her body. "And thank You, Lord, for… for light in the morning."

"No light in this hole."

Syntyche gasped. "Who…who's there?"

"Talk to yourself, do you?"

Since the stench of rotting excrement intensified, Syntyche guessed the person had moved closer. A cold finger poked her leg. She gagged as hot, sour breath enveloped her face.

"Stop. Who are you?" The tremble in her voice was unmistakable.

"Don't matter. What'd you do? Poison your man?"

"No. No, I'm a widow."

The cackling roughened into coughing.

She shrank back from the spray. "No. He died. I mean, I'd never k-kill someone." She gulped. "Did you?"

"Don't matter." The sharp finger poked harder. "What'd you do?"

Syntyche's voice squeaked. "I'm a follower of the Lord Jesus Christ, and I was telling someone in the marketplace about Him. I guess the storekeeper didn't like it—said I was a nuisance."

"Disturbing the peace, were you?"

"Bringing peace." Syntyche grimaced at the sharp edge of her retort. "Jesus brings peace and hope."

The person spit. Syntyche hoped it did not land on her clothes.

"My name is Syntyche."

"Name don't matter."

"It does to me. Since it's just us in this prison, it'd be nice to know your name."

"Hagne."

The women sat in silence until Hagne's stomach growled and Syntyche's answered.

"Guess we're both hungry. Hagne, how long have you been in here?"

"Don't know. Month. Maybe two or three. Maybe more."

Why was Hagne imprisoned? Syntyche decided against asking. Maybe she didn't want to know.

"Hagne, have you heard of Jesus of Nazareth?"

"No. Don't want to, neither."

Syntyche cradled her head on her arms. She'd try again tomorrow and the next day, for however long it took for Hagne to hear. This is why she'd been arrested, to share the love of Jesus with Hagne. Content, she slept.

Euodia slept until noon, waking only for a sip of water. She'd have slept later, but Claudia padded into the room with a basin of water and noisily plunked it on the stand.

"Master Marcellus will be in the garden in an hour."

Suddenly fully awake, last night's storm assailed her—Valeria, Syntyche, scrutinization, sneers, the presentation of a Juno statue, the Lord's guidance, Atticus's approval, Marcellus's request to talk.

She curled into a ball and pulled the cover over her head. "Go away."

Claudia tugged the cover away and tsked. "You didn't uncoil your hair or even undress? Get up. It will take a long time to untangle that snarl."

Audacious servant. Amelia's servants wouldn't dare speak that way.

Euodia sat up and yawned. "I was tired. I'm still tired. You don't understand."

Claudia had the good sense to pinch her lips closed.

Washed, hair brushed, wearing fresh clothes, Euodia scooped up Linus for an outside romp. Releasing him to play in the garden, she paused at its entrance, the heavy fragrance of roses swirling in the breeze and the drone of bees soothing last night's tension and today's uncertainty.

She searched for Marcellus, her heart fluttering in tremulous anticipation—he'd been somehow different last night—or did her heart quiver in fear of what he might say? She half hoped he'd been called away, thus postponing their talk. Anticipation battled dread. Dread won.

Had his parents demanded he divorce her? Would he forbid her ever again seeing her sister? Command her to break fellowship with other believers? Insist she pay homage to Juno? Berate her for Syntyche's actions?

Syntyche! She snapped off the head of an aging rose and rubbed it between her fingers until a small pile of bruised petals surrounded her toes. How to have her sister released from prison?

"Lord, help! What do I do? Will she forgive me if I help her, or will Juno's feast always stand between us no matter how I try to mend our relationship?"

A tug at her skirt stopped her pacing. Twisting to loosen the fabric of her dress from a curved thorn, she pricked her finger. Wincing, she stuck it in her mouth to stop the bleeding.

Had her sister been flogged? Euodia shuddered, unwilling to imagine the pain. If the prick of a single rose thorn hurt, how much worse a leather strap? More than once she'd tended slashed backs. If not cared for properly, infected wounds could kill.

Shaking her head—hard—refusing the image of her sister dead, a curl fell loose. She tucked it behind her ear the way Syntyche—more mater than sister—had done when she was a little girl. "You took such good care of me then. Now I will take care of you, but oh, Synee, how could you have let this happen to you? Will you never learn?"

She groaned in frustration. Tymon would be tight-lipped with anger. Would he pay to free their sister and redeem the family's honor? Or Clement? She knew Clement cared for Syntyche more than as a sister in Christ. If he refused, Brother Syzygus might help. He was a true Philippian like her and Syntyche—not Roman like Clement. He'd know someone to advise her how much bribe was required—he'd spoken of surviving life's harshness.

A marble bench graced the end of the garden path. Euodia ambled toward it. She plucked off the head of the rose closest to her. If Marcellus did not arrive soon, she'd order a carriage and begin the task of asking for help with Syntyche, and while she was out, she'd visit the wife of a young man in the private prison for debtors.

"Euodia."

Marcellus hurried down the path, a spring in his step she'd not realized had been missing. "I was studying the accounts to determine if we could spare the funds. We have plenty." His eyes shone like a child presenting a gift.

She stared at him blankly. Accounts? Funds? Why did he tell her this? She did not handle accounts. She placed orders, and Marcellus—or someone—paid the merchants.

"Oh. All right. That's good."

Marcellus's lips parted in a broad smile. "You don't understand, do you? We have the funds to free your sister." He laughed. "Close your mouth, Euodia."

"You will pay the bribe? Really? Oh, Marcellus!" She jumped to her feet and wrapped her arms around him. "Thank you. I never imagined...never thought to... You are so good to me."

"Even Pater agreed I should do this, although not for the same reasons I have. He cannot tolerate the stigma of family in prison."

"That you would do this for me!" His face blurred before her teary eyes.

Marcellus pulled her down to sit beside him on the bench. "Euodia, I do this for more than my love for you."

"Yes. I understand it is shameful for your—"

"It is not that." He cupped the back of his neck with a low groan. "It's the feast and then Pater's order, and, well, I know Mater is not easy to please, and the way you…despite their disapproval. Juno's statue convinced me too."

His faltering speech and broken thoughts puzzled her. Marcellus spoke with flawless eloquence. Always.

She searched for other signs of apoplexy.

"Marcellus, does your head hurt? Can you see me? Are you dizzy?"

He cocked his head. "Of course I see you, and yes, my head hurts. I've been doing calculations for hours. You know I'd rather be painting than counting beads on an abacus."

That sounded more like Marcellus.

He leaned forward, rested his forearms on his knees, and clasped his hands. "I'm trying to explain my decision."

She swallowed. Now would come the censure. Imagining contact forbidden with Syntyche nearly doubled her over in pain, but to be denied fellowship and worship with other believers… She covered her mouth to still her trembling chin, to hold in protests and words better left unsaid. Whatever happened, her sister would be free. She'd accept any cost Marcellus exacted.

Years of discipline brought her to prayer despite the grief piercing her mind.

Lord, help me reflect You.

Marcellus clasped and unclasped his hands. "I've watched you, and though I know you will not like it, had you watched."

She blanched. He knew of her mercy visits and use of household coins to ease the hurt of others. No wonder he could not speak with ease. He was furious.

"For years, I thought your service to the Jesus believers was a way to amuse yourself or to alleviate your guilt over having more wealth than most Philippians. Attending the sick and praying with your friends brought smiles to your face, and since you enjoyed it, I remained silent and did not interfere. Then Mater and Pater insisted on this feast, and it changed everything."

Throat tight, swallowing impossible, head pounding, she waited. Linus whimpered at her feet. She reached to comfort him, curling her fingers in his thick fur.

Marcellus stood. Paced. Sat. Faced her.

"I informed you of the feast, and you acquiesced to me without protest. You did not revile Pater but honored his command. You were not sullen with Mater and behaved with wisdom and grace when the statue was unveiled. Why? Or rather, how?"

Puzzled, she studied his face. There was no anger, only curiosity and—did she imagine it?—hunger.

"My Lord Jesus. Each time, I asked for wisdom, and He guided me."

"What was the cost of this God's attention, the payment for His response? More time with the ill? A votive? A sacrifice?"

Lord, guide me now.

"The cost is my obedience to Him, the surrender of my will." Her lips curved up. "I am well able to argue and pout and react poorly, if you didn't know."

He ran his fingers through his hair. "I do know. This time you didn't react that way, and through the years you have more and more often responded with gentleness." He pinned her with his eyes.

"This is because of your faith?"

"This is because as I remember to seek His guidance and obey, you see my Lord Jesus more easily."

"Euodia, I don't understand what or who changed you so that you respond with dignity and kindness, but I see it. I see something different, something I've decided I want to know more about if you will tell me."

"T-tell you? About…about Jesus?"

Abashed, he dipped his head, as if requesting something outlandish.

"Yes! Yes, of course. It has been my heart's desire to tell you of Him." Flustered, Euodia gathered her thoughts, surprised it was hard to share with a loved one.

"I will explain it as Syntyche does. Darkness covered the souls of all people. Fathomless darkness—"

"No. Tell me your story."

Euodia closed her eyes, searched for words. "Darkness covered *me.* Fathomless darkness lived in me, surrounded me—darkness so comfortable and familiar, I did not recognize it for what it was."

He leaned forward. "I see that darkness in myself. It's like a fog, impossible to penetrate."

"Our parents had died, and Tymon and Syntyche cared for me tenderly. I was loved, protected, often indulged. I was an easy child, quick to obey and eager to please, but always there was a niggling doubt that if I rebelled or if they knew all my thoughts and selfish deeds, they would find me unacceptable, stop loving me, stop caring for me."

"You are very easy to love, Euodia."

"What if I had not been?" She shrugged. "But I was compliant and did everything possible to earn their love. That fear of being unwanted or too much of a bother never stopped. I knew if I failed to keep their goodwill, their love, I had no one—a heavy burden for a child and a youth."

"Even a grown man. I've wondered that too. If I did not honor Pater, would he…" He grimaced.

"Your parents love you, Marcellus, as did mine, as did my siblings. But it's not enough—not for me. Something inside of me yearned to be known, completely known and still loved despite being known. My Lord Jesus loves me so much He forgave my sins and died for me. He took the punishment I deserved."

His guffaw startled Linus to bark in alarm. "You deserve no punishment. What did you ever do wrong?"

She hung her head. "Attitude. Greed. Pride."

He shifted away, narrowing his eyes. "Not so bad. Seems normal. You're human."

"And He is God. He's perfect. Anything less than perfection comes between me and the Almighty. It is sin."

Marcellus stood. "Your God is unreasonable. No one can be perfect."

"Except the Son of God. He is perfect, and He died to clear away my sins." Euodia fisted her hands. "Syntyche explains it better."

"I'm trying to understand how this changed you, what it means to you, not her." He resumed his seat, stretched his legs out, and leaned down to scratch Linus's head. "I knew your God died, and there were rumors He returned to life."

"Not rumors. Truth. Hundreds of people—more than just His followers—saw Him after His resurrection. Later, I will tell you the story of Jesus's birth and time on earth and the promises of God."

"Fine. Did you see Him? No? Then how do you know who this Jesus really is?"

"It's complicated."

"I'm listening."

She watched his ink-stained fingers ruffle Linus's fur. More often, they were paint-stained, the paint having seeped beneath his nails or dried in the creases of his hands. If she could paint a picture to help him see what it was like to know Jesus, he'd understand how He had changed her.

Lord?

She spoke slowly, holding his gaze. "Your paintings amaze me. Your gift, the way you select a brush and a color and then sweep them across a parchment or a wall so beautiful images appear is something I could never do. I watch in awe when you paint flowing rivers lined with slender reeds that seem to sway in the breeze or animals so vivid their eyes gleam with fury or people so real I stop to hear what they are saying. I could watch you create for hours. It is who you are."

His eyes softened. A smile curved his lips. "It is who I am."

"Loving us is who God is."

Eyes pensive, he allowed one short nod as if giving permission for her to continue.

"Your brush and paint and surface have no choice but to submit to your touch and your will. The results are magnificent, splendid images. When I choose to submit to my Lord's will, He uses me to create the beauty of kindness or patience."

Marcellus looked past her into the distance.

"Honestly, Marcellus, I do not understand it all. But when I trust Him, I am different. This is how I know He lives, having never seen Him, and how I know He's a God of love. And since He paid such a high price for me—the death of His Son—I must be of immense value to Him, too precious to abandon."

She strained to hear his murmured words. "A love you can rest in."

"Without fear of not being good enough." She chuckled. "He already knows I'm not and never will be good enough."

She waited, hands open on her lap. A tear eased down his face, catching in the prickles of his close-cropped beard. Euodia did not blink.

"How?"

His whispered question was, to her ears, a cymbal of gladness.

"Have you done wrong, Marcellus? Tell Him. Ask for forgiveness from the Savior. Ask Him to be Lord of your life."

"That's all?"

"That's the easy part. The hard part is remembering to ask for guidance and then obeying—doing what He says, going where He leads."

"One single God?"

"One."

"Pater and Mater…"

"They might never understand. I feared you would not. We will ask the Lord to enter your parents' lives."

Marcellus propped his elbows on his knees and laced his hands behind his head. His hair stood on end with endearing messiness.

"Yes."

Heart quickening, she felt joy surge through her. Words of praise and thanksgiving tumbled over each other so quickly she could not capture one to utter it aloud.

She reached for his hands. Wetting them with tears, she brought them to her lips. He rested his head against hers until Linus's warning growl broke the peace. Atticus advanced down the path.

"Marcellus, leave immediately. It is urgent you secure her sister's release. There are rumors of pestilence. If the guard flees, his replacement may not agree to the release."

Marcellus squeezed her hands. "We will talk more when I return."

When Marcellus disappeared into the house, Atticus pivoted to stand in front of her. He gazed down his long nose.

"You do not deceive me. You are displeased and offended with the gift of Juno's statue in spite of your pretense last evening."

She met his gaze without flinching. "I am. Yet I spoke truth. You are a generous man, and it is a beautiful work of art."

Again, she sensed his approval.

"You are a woman of wisdom, Daughter. Marcellus did well to choose you despite your erroneous beliefs."

Atticus turned with military precision and strode away. When he was out of sight, her legs gave way. She sat with a thump.

Syntyche scratched. Fleas, she hoped, not lice.

"Hagne, I need water." Her voice rasped. "When will there be more?"

"When they remember."

Syntyche seized the opening despite her parched throat. "One always remembers us. Our names are written on the palm of His hand."

"I don't want to hear no more about that God of yours."

Her lips curled in a tired smile. In another hour, she'd mention Him again. Simple protests, even vigorous protests did not deter her. Silently she offered praise that neither she nor Hagne could escape. Hagne's resistance already weakened. She'd stay here and pray for Hagne until the Lord Himself released her.

Please, Lord. Draw her to You.

Every flea bite, every throb of her head from hunger and thirst was worth the discomfort if another person came to faith. Paul had suffered here and still obeyed the leading to return to Philippi. He had spoken pointedly to her, ignoring her reluctance and protests. Had he not, she'd still be lost in darkness thicker than this cell. She could withstand a throbbing head and bug bites to speak truth to Hagne. She sneezed.

Men's voices rumbled outside the door. A chain rattled. Daylight blinded her.

"You. Come here."

Which "you" did he mean? Her or Hagne? Syntyche's eyes refused to open in the punishing brightness. A hand grabbed her arm, hauled her to her feet, and then dragged her outside into more light.

Now would come the flogging. She swayed.

Lord, be my strength.

"You're free to go." The guard shoved her. Falling on her hands and knees, she retched, the dry heaves producing nothing but pain in her parched throat. Blood welled from the cut in her lip.

Someone—her sight still blurred from the abruptness of dark to light—inserted his body between her and the guard. "Cease! She is no longer your prisoner."

"Keep her out of trouble and off the streets, or next time she'll stay till she's gnarled and gray."

Marcellus squatted beside her. "Syntyche. Let me help you up. I have a carpentum waiting to take you to your brother's or to my house, where Euodia will care for you."

"I cannot leave Hagne..."

"Another prisoner? I can do nothing for her. The bribe was for you alone."

Bribe? The release did not come from the Lord? Who dared interfere with her witness to Hagne? She was not supposed to be free until she'd given Hagne a glimpse of the Lord's mercy.

Marcellus lifted her into the carriage and tucked a blanket around her. A flask lay on the seat. "Euodia guessed you'd be chilled and not have been given food or water. She sent bread also but no cloths to stanch bleeding."

Hoarse, she spoke as few words as possible. "Her idea?"

"Freeing you from prison? Yes." Marcellus climbed aboard and tapped the roof. The carriage moved forward.

"Bribed?"

"The bribe was her idea, my pater's doing."

Syntyche shivered, forced words through the pain. "Go back. Hagne needs the Lord."

"Eat, Syntyche. You're sick, not able to help even yourself until you are cared for. There is sickness in the city. You need care so that you do not succumb to it. Do you want to be taken to your home or to my home?"

"Mine."

The carpentum stopped at her brother's house. Marcellus lifted Syntyche, pushed open the door, and carried her into the house. He sent one wide-eyed servant for Tymon and another for basins of water.

"Your room?"

She glanced toward the left and nodded when he paused at her door. He settled her on a hard chair.

Tymon stormed into the room, his eyes sweeping over Syntyche before facing Marcellus. "What have you and Euodia done to my sister?"

"Rescued her from prison."

Tymon's gaze shot to Syntyche. "Is this true?"

She nodded then closed her eyes, too weary to shield herself from Tymon's censure or offer the explanations he'd demand. The rawness of her throat and fear for Hagne's darkness consumed the little energy remaining to her.

The men left the room when servants entered with water and towels. Marcellus would give the facts he had to her brother. Did he know she'd been witnessing when she'd been arrested? She'd not hide the information even if her brother forced her to leave. She'd go…somewhere. The warm water soothed the bites and scratches. The women still cleaned her skin as she fell asleep.

She woke to Euodia's bloodshot eyes studying her face. The sisters stared without speaking until Syntyche coughed. With practiced assurance, Euodia slipped her arm behind her sister's back and helped her to sit and drink until the coughing stopped and Syntyche caught her breath.

"You have no faith."

Euodia looked at her as if she were the dog with three heads. She pressed the back of her hand against Syntyche's forehead.

Syntyche pulled away. "I'm not feverish."

"Since the pestilence has returned and you are talking like a madwoman, I needed to check."

"Why did you free me, Euodia?"

"Why did I… Are you serious? You were in prison for a week. You are my sister. Why would I not free you?"

"You stole the chance for me to witness to a woman in darkness."

"I gave you the chance to stay alive and witness to others."

"Go away, Euodia."

Euodia obeyed without hesitation. Syntyche quelled the sense she'd made a huge error by telling her sister to leave.

CHAPTER TEN

March

Rain poured through the atrium's open ceiling into the rainwater pool centered beneath it.

Occasionally, a gust of wind splashed water over the sides, turning the surrounding tiles slippery.

The chill in the air came not only from the brisk breeze accompanying the downpour.

Euodia sat opposite Syntyche and Malitta, waiting for Helena and Brother Clement to join them. She stared fixedly at her hands, refusing to interact with either woman. Averting her eyes did not limit her hearing.

Malitta jangled her bracelets. "I heard the most absurd rumor from Valeria—not a bit of truth to it. Funny, actually."

"Gossip does not interest me," Syntyche snapped.

"Nor me. But is it gossip if I tell the one who it is about so she can deny it publicly? Of course, if you'd rather not know…"

Syntyche's conviction against gossip faltered. "What is it? Tell me."

The bracelets jangled. Euodia imagined Malitta scooting forward.

"Those three weeks no one saw you—it's rumored you were in prison and then recovering from the ordeal."

"I was. Imprisoned for one week, recovering from the ordeal for two."

"No!"

Malitta's gasp almost broke Euodia's resolve to ignore the women. Discreetly, she leaned forward to hear Syntyche's explanation.

"So, it *is* true."

Malitta sounded half-delighted, half-horrified.

"It was an honor to know my witness so threatens idol worshipers that they removed me to silence my words."

"But to be arrested, imprisoned. Syntyche, how humiliating."

"I even shared Christ with another prisoner until I was forced to abandon her."

Pride tinged Syntyche's voice.

"Who forced you to leave?"

"My own sister."

Euodia caught her tongue between her front teeth and bit down. She would not be lured into this conversation. It did not involve Malitta. It should remain between her and her sister.

Brother Clement, his hair damp as if he'd just come from outside, ambled forward, his arms outstretched in welcome. "Sisters. Greetings in the name of the Lord. Thank you for meeting with me on this stormy day. Others have gathered in the kitchens—many from your baking classes, Syntyche—but I needed to speak with you two first. As usual, you will be in charge of the others."

His voice gentled. "There is another reason, Syntyche, that concerns you alone, but I believe you will appreciate your sister and friend being here."

Euodia looked up, focused on his face.

"You may have heard we face a crisis with the return of the pestilence. It strikes the weakest among us—our children, the elderly, those recovering from other illnesses, but not them only. It's been observed that those who work near the remaining marshes and breathe its vapors frequently become ill. As you are aware, we cannot predict who will sicken yet recover, or who will succumb to it."

Malitta stood. "Forgive me. I just remembered a promise it is imperative I keep." Snatching her palla, she hurried from the house into the rain without covering her head or shoulders.

For the length of one breath, the sisters' eyes met and held. Malitta had made no promise. Fear of sickness drove her into the rain.

And the new bits of gossip she'd eagerly share.

Clement's words revealed that he too understood Malitta's sudden departure. "My beloved sisters, you are faithful no matter what trials we face. Brother Syzygus and I thank God you work alongside us as you did with the Apostle Paul."

Clement bowed his head then turned to Syntyche. "Sister, of all of us, this will be most difficult for you. Whatever you decide will be respected. I understand if this request provokes too much heartache…."

"How may we serve our Lord?" Syntyche's voice was warm and soft—a rarity.

Euodia noted a look linger between them.

"Mater and I have gathered fruits and a supply of wormwood for tea. Euodia, you know how to administer it. You can teach Syntyche how to help you."

From the corner of her eye, Euodia saw her sister stiffen.

Clement tilted his head to look through the rainwater opening in the ceiling. "It is cold and rainy outside, but there are many who suffer and need our help. Will you go with me now to ease their misery?"

The sisters stood and spoke simultaneously. "Yes."

Euodia clamped her jaws together. If Syntyche said one more word, pushed one more time for a dying person to accept Jesus and be saved, she'd drag her sister outside, bolt the door, and leave her standing in the downpour. Why had her sister come here with all the memories it would stir?

She sprinkled wormwood powder into a cup of warmed water then spooned it between the lips of the gaunt woman. Red streaks where the woman had scratched at insect bites lined her thin arms. The scratching began again. Wishing she had lavender oil, and surrounded by the acrid odor of loose bowels and air soured by the stench of poverty, Euodia thanked God she had a strong stomach. She'd change the bedclothes when the woman's chills passed.

She knew being here and seeing this was hard for Syntyche. If only she'd hush her preaching and use her hands to help. Thankfully, Sister Cora was here and anticipated the need for more water and cleaning cloths. She'd noticed Cora looking at Syntyche askance when she refused to stop talking.

"Cora, my sister and I are going to the next house. Will you stay and watch over this woman?"

At Cora's nod, she gathered her supplies and tapped Syntyche's shoulder. Outside, she turned to her sister. "Syntyche, this is not the same as with your Alex. Let them recover before you preach."

"It's exactly the same. You'd let them die before knowing Christ—like Alex did." Rain—or were they teardrops?—dripped off Syntyche's chin.

Euodia leaned forward. "I'm trying to keep them alive."

Thunder rumbled nearby. Syntyche spoke over it. "I'm trying to give them the hope of eternal life while there is time."

Euodia grasped Syntyche's arm. "Please, listen to me. There is a time to heal and a time to teach."

She jerked away from her sister's grip. "They can hear the teachings while they heal."

Frustration raised Euodia's voice. "They cannot hear you when they are so ill."

"They will not hear me at all if they are dead." Syntyche jammed her hands on her hips.

Euodia swiped the rain from her nose.

"No one can help hearing you. You never listen. You never stop talking."

"And you have such little faith and so much fear that you never give voice to the Lord's promises."

"I am working to serve the Lord, not my pride as you are, Syntyche."

"You work to receive approval from those who think you so sweet. I know better. I raised you."

"I do not—"

"Sisters!" Clement's fury was unmistakable.

An audience of six stared at them.

Syntyche stripped off her sodden clothes and left them on the floor. Once she was dry and warm, she'd wring them out and hang them to dry. She toweled her hair, brushed it, dressed warmly, and returned to the pile of wet clothes. Their dampness had spread into a puddle, leaving more mess to clean. She picked up her palla, squeezing it bit by bit until more water puddled on the floor and the cloth was wrinkled and twisted, wrung out.

Wrung out—exactly how she felt after today and the memories of Alex's death.

Yes, three people came to faith today, but two died as she spoke—if only she'd been there sooner.

She pressed her dripping under-tunic in a towel to remove some of the water. Euodia had yelled at her—a first.

She squeezed out a stream of water from her stola, hearing again Clement's public disapproval and anger when he'd ordered them to return to his house.

His words and evident disappointment stung. He shouldn't have spoken to her or Euodia that way, accusing them of causing trouble and hurting the witness of the believers. Obviously he hadn't prayed before reprimanding them. Euodia had left his house in tears. Not her—she'd been furious. How dare he undermine her work?

She flung her sandals in the fire and listened to them splutter. They were soaked beyond saving, maybe like her work for the Lord. The expressions of shock and judgment from the other women and Clement would never fade from her mind.

She sank to her knees amid the clothes on the floor and dropped her head in her hands. More than anything, would the horror of Alex's death ever wane?

Alex—her beautiful, strong husband. Felled by the evil air. *Mal aria* the Romans called the sickness. "Roman fever" her people named it. He'd complained of a headache—he who never complained, never seemed to suffer aches no matter how hard he worked or how scarce his sleep.

Soon he tossed on their bed, shoving away the covers or pulling them tight as he alternated between short bouts of chills and hours of fever, too sick to keep food down. Exhausted after two weeks of tending her weakening husband, she'd fallen asleep by his side—waking to find her Alex lifeless, lost to her forever. Without warning—wife to widow.

Though her heart yet ached, she shed no tears—none were left.

Euodia's swollen eyes could not be disguised. Claiming a headache—which was true—she planned not to leave her room. She startled at a tap on her door, the movement causing sharp pains in her head. Before she could refuse anyone admittance, the door opened.

Malitta stood silhouetted in the doorway. Few sights would have been more unwelcome.

"Euodia?" Malitta peered into the darkened room. "I heard all about it and came to comfort you."

"I don't feel well. Could you return another time?"

"Of course you don't feel well after brawling in public with your sister. I'm shocked at the horrible lies she said. I'd never repeat them to anyone, and naturally I don't believe a word you're rumored to have said, although I've heard others believe them."

Malitta threw aside a pillow and thumped herself onto the bed. Euodia gritted her teeth as the mattress bounced.

"I won't stay long. You sound terrible. There is one more thing you need to know besides that most people believe you wronged Syntyche. Helena confided it in me."

"If it's confidential she wouldn't want it shared, so please don't—"

"Clement was so upset last night that he went to discuss it with Brother Syzygus."

Euodia grimaced. "That's understandable. We were all upset."

"They wrote Paul."

Euodia's heart sank. Paul would hear of last night's travesty. Tears of shame scalded her cheeks.

Lord?

Joy.

Joy? She must have misunderstood—or He had.

She sniffled. "Malitta..."

"They sent it this morning with a small group led by Ephi... Epheditus...Ediph—"

"Epaphroditus."

"Paul is in Rome, yes?" Malitta tapped her chin. "Six weeks there, six weeks back if all goes well. We'll know whose side Paul is on in a few months."

"Side?" Euodia sighed. Malitta needed to leave. "Please hand me a basin. I think I'm going to be sick."

"I really must go, but I'll send a servant to you."

With a whirl of fabric and the jingling of her bracelets, Malitta slammed the door. Euodia caught her breath as another pain stabbed her head. She winced at its intensity. Needing a basin was likely true. She reached for the vial beside her bed and rubbed lavender oil on her temples.

As the throbbing eased, she returned to the Lord's word. Joy?

"Lord, really?"

Joy.

"Lord, the last thing I feel is joy. Shame. Self-disgust—how could I say or even think such horrid words to my sister? And I'm angry she doesn't understand how abrasive she can be. Those poor people are so sick, and sometimes their eyes glaze over while she's teaching. If they're not hearing and learning, then she's just talking—not teaching."

"I know." She groaned. "We're talking about me, not her. Fine. Joy. There is no joy in yesterday's calamity."

She covered her face, inhaled the oil lingering on her fingertips. She'd often used lavender to soothe burns and headaches. It was reputed to bring a sense of peace and well-being.

Now she used it because she liked the fragrance, but before she'd come to faith, she'd applied it to her hair rinses and to her bath in her longing for tranquility. The gentle scent helped, true, but nothing compared to knowing the Lord, depending on His strength when she was weak or needed serenity.

Yesterday she'd not turned to Him for strength when her temper rose. She'd weakened after years—a lifetime of years—of restraining her words, biting her tongue, dipping her head, and saying nothing. The barrier broken, was she strong enough to repair the rupture or even build a wobbly bridge? She'd laugh at the absurdity if moving didn't hurt so much.

My power is made perfect in your weakness.

She bolted upright. Pain pierced her head. Immediately she lay down.

That teaching from the Lord—Clement read it a few months ago during worship when the church in Corinth shared a copy of Paul's letter. Now the Lord had given the reminder to her.

Twice, she whispered the words aloud.

His power. Images of the sea crashing on the shores of Neapolis, the music of a wren, of the star-strewn sky and lightning's brilliance. More magnificent than all of those was the change she'd seen in Cerberus and herself and so many others.

Made perfect. Perfection. Flawless. It was inconceivable. Trying to imagine the impossible, she shook her head and regretted the movement.

In my weakness. She could provide plenty of weakness.

His power. Made perfect. In her weakness.

Maybe joy could come from yesterday.

Hope began to heal, and peace—beyond that of a lavender bouquet—eased her to sleep.

Syntyche tucked in the end of the braided bread. An egg wash and a sprinkle of sesame seeds after it baked, and it would be ready to serve along with the baklava and meringue cookies she knew Tymon favored. She hoped his mouth would be too full to reprimand her when he returned tonight. At least the pastries would remind him how he enjoyed her baking, and he'd hesitate before casting her out.

His steward had informed her that Ty left on a business trip the morning after she'd been released from prison. She and Ty had not spoken since her arrest. If he discovered that since recovering she daily spoke with the sick and dying of the mal aria, he'd order her to stop.

Her refusal would infuriate him. She dusted her floured hands together to loosen the powder. Somehow she must continue those visits.

Ahh. She'd mention that Euodia also tended the ill, even holding their heads while they sipped her tinctures, and she cleaned the filth from their bodies. That would distract him from her visits.

No need for him to know they no longer worked together. He'd barrage her with a series of questions she'd prefer to avoid.

Flour covered the surface of her table. She brushed it into a pile and set the spices and butter to one side. Her baking was complete, but the students would soon arrive for their lesson and to hear the Lord's teachings—if any of them still wanted to learn from her.

Last week, only two had come. She suspected they'd not yet heard of the debacle with Euodia.

Anger raised its irrational head. Clement had not sent an apology. Euodia had offered no gesture to show she was contrite. Only Malitta had visited to offer her support and share her dismay over Euodia's accusations. She'd appreciated knowing several of the other women were shocked by Euodia's behavior. It had been a pleasant visit until Malitta shared Helena's confidence about the letter written to Paul.

Breaking trust did not sit well with her, and this was the second time Malitta had shared private information. True, both times it had been to her—the concerned person—but still… She'd need to watch her words around the woman.

It was a relief Paul would be told of Euodia's disrespect. If Paul sent a private word, maybe Euodia would realize how wrong she was and work on her failures. She hurt the church and its ministry with her timidity in witnessing.

A little kitchen maid with curly hair scurried to the table, gathered the flour-crusted bowls and sticky utensils to scour clean. Syntyche watched her, wondering what her name was. Euodia would have known and greeted her. The maid was new, probably not a believer. Before she could beckon the girl closer, Malitta walked into the kitchen.

"No one came to the door, so I let myself in. I knew you wouldn't mind."

"I don't, but if my brother were here, he'd not be pleased. He guards his privacy."

"Tymon isn't here?"

Puzzled, Syntyche cocked her head. "How do you know my brother's name?"

Malitta's eyes shifted. "You must have mentioned it. You're my dearest friend, so we talk about everything."

Hardly! Syntyche didn't think she'd mentioned his name but didn't want to argue. "Are you here for baking lessons?"

"Lessons? No. My slaves don't have enough to do. I'd not dream of taking on their menial work so they can laze more than they already do."

Did Malitta have any idea she'd insulted her "dearest friend"?

"What do you need, Malitta?" Syntyche heard the ire in her voice that Malitta probably did not. Tired from the morning's work and needing to freshen her appearance before Ty returned, she felt her patience quickly disappearing.

She beamed. "There's a group of us—we call ourselves Syntyche's Voice—who want to learn boldness from you and speak for you. We don't want to be anything like that Euodia." She giggled. "Oh, I forgot she's your sister."

Speechless, Syntyche stared at Malitta. When words finally formed, she spoke slowly so Malitta would understand.

"Euodia is my sister—my beloved sister. We may disagree, but I would do anything for her and she for me."

"If you think so, but I heard she's planning—"

"I do think so. Further, I cannot teach boldness, only encourage you to seize every chance to share our Lord's teachings."

Malitta pursed her lips.

"And lastly, you must disband this group of 'voices.' They are not mine. I speak for myself, and no one else can or should speak for me."

A voice from behind surprised her. "Syntyche needs no help in speaking for herself, never has." Tymon paused. "*Malitta?*"

Had he seen a ghost, his face would not be paler. "Malitta, what are you doing here? Synee, you know this woman?"

As pale as Ty's face was, Malitta's face was red.

Syntyche's gaze darted back and forth between them. Neither seemed pleased to see the other.

Fury brimmed from Tymon's eyes. "You. Leave my house. Do not return. Ever."

He shifted, his animosity and stance resembling a wild animal preparing to attack. He valued his privacy and could be as grumpy as a brown bear, but she'd never heard him speak with such loathing to anyone.

Malitta swiveled and sped out the door.

"You. I will speak with you in my office. Now."

Disconcerted, Syntyche followed without protest. Once in his office, he closed the door and swung to face her.

"I leave as you are released from prison and return to find that conniving woman in my house. Explain. Tell me."

For the second time in less than an hour, Syntyche struggled for words. Only one emerged.

"No."

She'd never seen someone turn purple or move so fast.

Ty bounded across the room until his nose almost touched hers. "You. Tell. Me."

He'd eaten garlic. She retreated a handsbreadth. Reconsidered. Relented.

"A merchant took offense to my conversation with a woman outside his shop, reported me as a nuisance, and had me arrested."

"That, I knew. What was that lying scum doing in my house? How do you know her? What did she tell you? Why would you associate with that vermin?"

Syntyche scrutinized her brother. It had been years since she'd seen him so angry—and that for a friend who'd been deceived by his betrothed.

"I met her when I worked at the baths. She's one of the wealthy ones—always wearing purple—who could visit often and linger." She frowned into eyes identical to her own. "She said I reminded her of someone and asked if I had a brother or sister. She meant you, didn't she, Ty?"

"What did she say to you?" Deep lines marred his forehead. "Tell me. All of it. What do you know about her?"

"Nothing. She's married. Wears a lot of scented ointments." She scrunched her nose. "Too many scents. Likes bracelets." She refrained from adding the other things she knew. *Breaks confidences. Mistakenly assumes I'm her best friend. Insults me.*

She took a deep breath. "She attends worship with Euodia and me. Sometimes she helps deliver baskets to the poor."

"A real Jesus person." He snorted. "More like a viper circling the feet of fools."

"You know her."

"A great misfortune in my life." Tymon rubbed his hand over his eyes. "Synee, stay away from her. She's a thief and a liar."

"Thief? No. Her husband is wealthy, very wealthy, and allows her to do as she pleases, purchase whatever she wants. She has no reason to steal."

He leveled his eyes with hers. "Little sister, a thief can steal what is much more valuable than jewels or gold. Trust me. Mattila is a thief—the worst kind."

CHAPTER ELEVEN

April, the First Sabbath

Euodia lingered, waiting for her sister. She enjoyed the hint of spring's warmth in the air, but she knew she'd be late if she waited any longer for Syntyche. She'd arrived at their meeting place early. If they could talk or at least hug, she'd be more confident about joining the others. Braving worship after the humiliation of a few weeks ago would be easier if she and her sister entered together.

She missed how Syntyche tried to restrain laughter when she should be solemn. She missed hearing her pray and her boldness in witnessing. She missed the shared looks when the same memory occurred to them both.

Syntyche must not be attending worship today, or perhaps she'd gone early to avoid her. Her throat swelled with grief. Again today, they'd not reconcile. Would they ever be close again?

Giving up, she hurried to join two women who welcomed her with hugs and soft smiles. Perhaps the incident had been forgiven or was not known by everyone. Perhaps she'd hidden away with Linus long enough for the scandal to pass.

Entering the worship service, she realized the hope was false. Confronted by averted eyes or unfriendly faces, her smiles met sneers. Her offered hand received a turned shoulder, her arms, a dodged hug. Despite the wall of hostility, she searched the group for Syntyche. Her sister would never stand against her.

Unexpectedly, the unfriendly faces became welcoming. Hands reached out, bypassing her, murmuring Syntyche's name and drawing her sister into their midst.

Euodia pressed a hand against the knot forming in her belly. At least Marcellus was not here to see this. His first impression of a group of Christ followers would have been so wrong. They were to be of one mind, not divided into factions and shunning a fellow believer.

"Don't mind them." Malitta's perfume announced her presence. "Syntyche gathered them to exclude you. I heard about it and went to her house to demand she stop her scheme. Come. I saved you a place."

It didn't sound like something Syntyche would do, but quite a few women had clustered around her. She grasped Malitta's arm.

"Dear friend, thank you for standing with me."

Worship began with prayers and praise. Brother Clement returned to his seat as Brother Syzygus shuffled forward with a parchment.

"Paul's letter to Thessalonica exhorts us to live in peace with one another." He bowed his head, then looked out over those gathered.

"To live in peace—a good thought, a worthy goal. We are all so different. How are we to do this? Paul tells us, and I believe he is led by the Holy Spirit in his letters to the churches. Warn those who are idle. Encourage the timid, help the weak, be patient with everyone. Make sure nobody pays back wrong for wrong, but always try to be kind to each other and to everyone else."

Hand trembling, he held out the letter for Clement to take and protect. "Idleness is not a problem for you, my friends. I know you work hard. You are encouragers, and most often you are patient."

Syzygus swayed slightly. He dabbed the corners of his mouth with a small cloth. "It is the last part of that instruction which weighs on my heart, where the Lord has revealed to me we as the church of Philippi struggle."

He opened wide his thin arms as if to embrace those who listened. "Kindness to each other is too often missing. That omission shouts loudly to those who watch and judge if our lives are changed enough that they want to know more of our Savior. Do we treat each other with love?"

Clement rose and moved forward. "Brother Syzygus, may I add to your message?"

Syzygus immediately nodded and sank into the closest seat.

"Kindness does not show itself in comparing or in controlling but with love. Remember in the first letter to Corinth, near the end, Paul described how love is expressed in actions...."

His voice dimmed as Euodia's thoughts turned inward. She'd prided herself on her thoughts and actions being kind—until they were not. Until exasperation with Syntyche spilled out of her mouth. Until Helena believed the worst of her and scolded her, and Clement reduced her to tears. Until resentment rubbed raw a blister as Amelia stayed and stayed and rearranged her home until it no longer seemed home. Until Atticus mentioned he prepared to return to the villa whether Amelia returned or not. Until women she'd believed to be steadfast sisters in the Lord turned away from her.

Malitta squeezed her arm.

Malitta was faithful even when her own sister betrayed her. She took a deep breath and coughed—all kind thoughts disappearing as the woman's cloying scent clogged her throat and nose so she couldn't breathe.

She eased away from Malitta to observe Syntyche. Was she listening to Paul's admonition or Syzygus's teaching? Of course not. She was looking at her hands. And no one described her sister as unkind, but the crowd of women surrounding her—had they ever been flayed with Syntyche's knife-edged tongue? Unlikely.

Fine. Syntyche might deceive for a while, but eventually, the others would realize that she, Euodia, was more Christlike. Kindly, she patted Malitta's musk-scented hand and bowed her head.

Syntyche walked as rapidly as possible without running. It had not been a good morning.

She'd stopped by the prison to take food to Hagne only to learn the pitiful woman had died. If she'd visited a few days before, maybe she could have helped her in some way. Again, she'd been too late to help someone she cared about.

She ran a few steps, walked, ran a few steps.

The day had started off wrong when the dough for Euodia's favorite pastry had been slow to rise. Foolishly she'd added too much sugar, which any baker knew slowed the dough's proving. Still, she'd been determined to take it to worship this morning as a peace offering. They'd had difficult times before but nothing like this. If it bothered her to be in a public spat, Euodia would be devastated.

She missed Euodia, missed seeing her single-dimpled smile and her eyes light up when surprised. She missed laughing over memories and sharing how the Lord moved in their lives.

She missed baking treats for her sister and preparing meals for both her siblings—rare since Euodia married Marcellus. She missed scolding Tymon for his odd humor and trying to hush Euodia's giggles. Those times had been stars in her sky.

Her mouth watered at the warm pastry's sweet smell. On the way to worship, they'd sample one together as they used to do. Perhaps it was time to share with Euodia her secret to the recipe. It was a special pastry—just for the two of them—one their mater had created.

She veered around a group of beggars, dodged a runaway dog, and sidestepped fresh evidence that a horse had recently clopped past. She was later than usual, but Euodia would wait for her. She always did.

She had not. Syntyche turned in a slow circle, searching the corners and shadows for her wisp of a sister and the brilliant blue scarf she wore to cover her hair on worship days. It had been their mater's, and her sister treasured it, saved it for special times. Nothing. No blue scarf. No sister. Euodia must be very ill, or still deeply embarrassed, to miss another worship service.

Maybe she should return and check on… A glimpse of blue caught her attention. The scarf had to belong to Euodia. She'd never seen anyone other than their mater with that exact color. Good. She was not ill or injured but… Of course, they hadn't spoken recently, but still…Euodia had not waited for her? She'd risen an hour early this morning to bake this treat for her sister. Ungrateful girl.

Fuming, she shoved the pastries into the outstretched hands of the closest beggar and set off toward the worship place.

The courtyard stood vacant except for a few individuals. Strange. Usually several of her friends waited for her outside the building.

Two women comforted their infants. Did they ignore her call of greeting or not hear her voice over the tiny squalls?

She nodded to an elderly man who might have turned his back or decided to go a different direction. Uneasy, she waved to a woman she'd led to faith and could think of no excuse for the glare she received. Her steps faltered. Had she become unwelcome here? Was she shunned for being arrested? Paul had been arrested, and no one turned their back on him.

She pushed open the door, searching for Euodia. Maybe she'd saved her a place. Maybe they could worship side by side and begin to heal.

Euodia's back was to her. The thin shoulders curled forward, and Syntyche realized Euodia faced an unfriendly group. Before she could intervene and stand in front of her sister as a buffer, the aloofness warmed to smiles and outstretched hands.

"Syntyche. We've been waiting for you."

The one who spoke—an unfamiliar face—gathered her into a hug. Several hugs, a few greetings, some assurances of welcome followed. She'd misread the ones in the courtyard. By the time she wiggled free and looked around, Malitta's arm circled Euodia's shoulders, leading her away.

Tymon's words rang in her mind. *"A thief can steal what is much more valuable than jewels or gold. Malitta is a thief—the worst kind."*

She shook her head to clear her mind. Malitta was not a thief. Malitta didn't steal Euodia from her. Euodia's own foolish fear and stubborn spirit kept them apart. When Euodia apologized, she'd graciously offer forgiveness.

Brother Clement began to speak. She listened, eyes lowered. She could not look at the man who so misjudged and shamed her. He too needed to express remorse—in public he should offer an apology to her for overreacting when she corrected her sister.

"Beloved, I do not have the letter to Corinth with me, but these words are seared in my mind, perhaps because I struggle with this." He raised his voice. "Love is not easily angered."

Syntyche hoped her sister was hearing his admonition. If Euodia had not become so upset while they cared for the mal aria victims, they'd have never fought.

She bowed her head lower. *Lord, open Euodia's ears to hear the correction You have for her.*

Afterward, the worshipers gathered in the courtyard before gradually dispersing. Syntyche knew the maters holding young children would leave first, the elderly members following soon afterward—probably eager for a nap. The single men and women would stroll as slowly as possible back to the city. The widows lingered longest before returning to loneliness.

Determined to avoid Clement until he appeared contrite, Syntyche joined the small circle—smaller than usual—of those who'd greeted her. These few understood she was a better witness than Euodia. From her viewpoint in the group, if Clement approached them, she'd see him in time to hurry away.

Surreptitiously, she searched for Euodia. There. She was leaving without speaking. Her blue scarf almost touched Malitta's vivid purple scarf, their heads so close together it reminded her of Cerberus and the meaning of his name. After Clement apologized, she'd ask if he'd heard from Cerberus.

If what Ty implied was true, her little sister was in danger. She huffed. Ty could be so dramatic. He and Malitta must have had a misunderstanding over a business matter that he continued to resent. Still, she'd ask a few questions, learn how they knew each other, and determine if Euodia should be warned.

CHAPTER TWELVE

May

Syntyche planned her query with care. With the wisdom of a woman who'd been a daughter, sister, and wife of a hungry man who was easily angered and who growled louder than his stomach if not well fed, Syntyche prepared a meal Ty would relish. The dishes scraped clean, he pushed them away, patted his trim belly and stretched.

"Excellent, Synee, an excellent meal like our mater's. Tell me, what do you want?"

She laughed. Ty knew her well. She'd not pretend to misunderstand.

"I want to know about Malitta."

His contentment vanished. "A poor way to end a fine meal."

"I cannot stop thinking of your words—that she is a thief and can steal things of more value than gold."

"Have you talked to her? Did she try to explain my reaction to seeing her here?"

"She attended worship, but I've not spoken with her." She supposed he'd want to know of Euodia's involvement with Malitta. After she understood Ty's attitude, if Malitta was a true threat, she'd tell him.

"As you will. Remember my friend Marcus? You were just a little girl, maybe nine..."

"Of course I remember Marcus—tall with such dark eyes. He always brought me a little gift, and he was deaf in one ear, right?"

"Yes. Marcus was my closest friend—an honest man, a Roman noble of the top tier and wealthy. Very wealthy." Ty looked past her, his eyes unfocused.

"Ty." She waved a hand in front of his face. "Malitta?"

He blinked.

"Malitta and I had been friends since childhood. At one time, our houses were side by side."

Had been friends? Syntyche narrowed her eyes in concentration. "I don't remember her or hearing her name."

"She was seldom mentioned in our home. Neither of our parents liked or trusted her. They never told me why. Anyway, I introduced her to Marcus. They fell in love, or so I thought. He told me he'd found the woman he'd dreamed of and never knew existed. Synee, are you certain you want to know this? It was a long time ago."

She stuck out her lower lip in a pout. "Not so long. I'm not that old."

"You're an ancient cranky crone." He feigned fear as she curled her fingers into claws.

"You've been married, so I'll speak candidly. Two things happened. Malitta, who proclaimed deep love for Marcus, was caught in an indiscretion. Marcus was devastated."

"Oh no. How could she... Wait. Was she willing or forced?"

"She boasted to a servant it was her choice and not the first time. She did not even care for the other man. In her words, he was a 'convenient distraction.'"

"Marcus must have been furious. No wonder you dislike her."

"No." His jaw tightened. His fists clenched and unclenched. Clenched and unclenched. A wave of uncertainty swept through her. She'd never seen him so angry.

"It is worse. She repulses me because of the other part she told the servant. She was in love with Marcus's wealth and standing—not him—and claimed no fault in her actions."

"She used him."

"She stole confidence and joy from him. She stole the courage to trust."

"That's why you said more valuable than jewels or gold."

"He left for Rome."

"Does he blame you, since you introduced them?"

Ty's eyes were hooded and bleak. "How could he not? I haven't heard from him in years."

"Ty, why did the servant tell you these things?"

He reached for the goblet and studied its design. "She and I were, um, friends."

Syntyche understood and ignored his discomfort. "Maybe she lied."

"I wondered that too and confronted Malitta, so not to repeat falsehoods. When I questioned her and after she finished screaming about the disloyalty of her servant, she confirmed it was true. Worse, she denied the responsibility of hurting him, insisted her behavior was normal. She never believed I'd go straight to Marcus. She thought my loyalty lay with her as a childhood friend."

His eyes bored into hers. "I refused to let the deception continue, no matter the cost, no matter who was hurt or what friendships I forfeited. She told her parents I lied and had ruined her chances to marry a wealthy noble. They withdrew their business and advised others to do the same. They moved away and let their house fall into disrepair. It hurt the value of our house too."

"I remember there were several hard years."

"We lost almost everything. Rumors were circulated about our integrity in our business dealings. We survived. I'm convinced it sped our pater to his grave and aged our mater thirty years. It was why your dowry was small. By the time Euodia married, the business recovered, and I could offer more."

"I never wanted to marry anyone but my Alex." She covered his clasped fists with her hand. "You did right to tell Marcus. Ty, I'm proud of you."

"You do what's right and good too. I'm proud of you, little Synee."

Her stomach soured. Her brother would not be proud if he knew her many deceptions.

Syntyche did not sleep well that night. She blamed the fish, the pillow, the warmth of the room, the snoring of the servant outside her door. She blamed the disconcerting news about Hagne's death and Malitta's deceptions. She blamed her concern over the order of kitchen supplies she needed to place. She blamed the wind's whistling and the hairpin she forgot to remove.

When morning peeped beneath the door, she slept and dreamed she was running naked through the crowded marketplace as Malitta pointed and laughed.

Pulling herself awake, she gulped in shuddering breath, her bedclothes soaked as if she had been running. Trembling, she reached for the cup of water by her bed.

Maybe she'd breathed the mal aria.

Maybe she too was a thief, deceiving her brother, stealing his trust.

Maybe, like Malitta, she believed her actions to be acceptable, her words unharmful.

Maybe she'd been working too hard.

Maybe she knew the truth and feared to admit it.

Euodia's fingers intertwined with Marcellus's—truthfully, a perfect fit. She loved the bounce in his step as he walked beside her. She loved his scent of paints and spices and his steady kindness. Theirs was a love match, advantageous to her alone. He'd defied his parents' objection to a Greek merchant's daughter and overcome her parents' objections to a Roman noble as a son-in-law.

Linus sniffed each plant, often stopping in front of them so suddenly they tripped. Such a pleasant day to stroll the gardens with her husband and their rambunctious pup. Maybe now was the time to once more broach the subject of telling others of his faith.

Her eyes caressed his face. Joined in marriage, joined in love, and joined in faith. How blessed she was. The only things more wonderful would be to have a child and to worship with Marcellus among other believers.

She tried again. "You say you are a Christ follower. When will you attend worship with me and let others share in our joy?"

He leaned over and tickled the soft spot behind her ear. "Hmm?"

Twirling away, she walked backward, holding him at arm's length. "Come with me next week."

She wanted to dance through the streets and proclaim to the world that Marcellus had come to faith. With him attending worship, they'd learn together and encourage each other, and she'd be focused on listening so they could discuss the teaching. Otherwise, she'd continue to think about Syntyche and wonder if they'd ever be close again.

"Next week, I'll be away. Remember I leave tomorrow."

"Then the next? Please?"

"Mater will still be here, maybe my pater too."

Puzzled, she stopped and scanned his eyes.

"Caught you!" His arm encircled her waist as if to pick her up.

Squealing, she twisted away as Linus returned, circling and whimpering to assure himself she was in no danger. "Hush, Linus. Marcellus, what difference does it make if your parents are still here?"

"Euodia, let's not talk about this now. Wait until I return."

She wrapped her fingers through his as they resumed walking. Marcellus was a man she'd believed unafraid to take a stand. Until now.

"You haven't told your parents, have you?"

His silence answered her. She'd questioned if they knew, had wondered if they'd hidden their displeasure, hoping he'd change his mind, thinking their opposition would entrench his decision. How foolish she was. Amelia was incapable of disguising her feelings, and Atticus would not have tried.

"Euodia, it would be embarrassing to them for their son to be a Christ follower only a few months after the banquet for Juno. You must realize it was a costly endeavor—even for them—and instead of being feted, they'd be ostracized, ridiculed to their faces and behind their backs. I can't do that to them."

"But you can turn your back on the Savior."

He winced. "I'm not turning my back on our Lord. I'm just not proclaiming my beliefs to everyone and offending my parents. I'm being diplomatic."

He stopped walking and nestled her hand against his warm chest. "If it is known I'm a believer, I will lose my commission with Rome. They will select a different artist—one who reveres the gods and pays homage to Caesar." He grimaced. "True, it's highly unlikely since I'm of the nobility, but I could be declared a traitor, and Rome is not known for her mercy. Do you see why I dare not be seen with a gathering of Jesus people? It could cost too much—relationships, family, career."

Cost too much? He spoke of a painting, not his life—not truly. "Marcellus, I..." How could she help him understand? His testimony could influence others—persuade them to at least hear the message of love and salvation. His reticence did nothing. Her heart thumped and skipped a beat.

She sounded like Syntyche. He sounded like—no. Not like her. She met with other believers. She did not consider the cost. She infused Christ's teachings discreetly, in a subtle, gentle manner that was never offensive.

Or noticed.

"Once I'm established, an in-demand artist with Rome, I can worship our Lord as long as it's not noticed and I'm sensible, not blatantly defying Rome. Then I will be diligent in handling my beliefs discreetly as you do."

She cringed as his words echoed hers.

"I know you understand, Euodia. You're not at all like your sister. You did not defy my parents over Juno. You went along with it as if you approved, and you did this willingly."

His accusation stung. He was correct, and he was so wrong.

"I did not do that of my own volition. No, I took each matter before the Lord and followed His leading to live in peace and unity." She slipped her hand from his, paced away, and returned.

"Dearest, at times, in being diplomatic, in being so compliant, I felt the traitor. I did not understand His leading but trusted Him to bring good of what He guided me to do." She cupped his face with her hands. "Your faith is the good He brought. Had I not obeyed His guidance, it may have damaged my witness to you."

"I am glad you obeyed." He kissed the top of her head. "Euodia, for now, isn't it enough to ask the Lord for guidance? To worship in private? To just live differently as you do?"

She blinked. Is this how she appeared to others? Content to live differently but not speak her beliefs?

Lord?

Realization flooded her. Not since the public confrontation with her sister had she asked for the Lord's guidance. Her tear-filled eyes met her husband's gaze.

"Dearest Marcellus, you must ask the Lord these questions, not me. And then you must obey His leading, not my example."

Syntyche's boldness frightened her—it always had. To be like her sister was impossible, but did she hide behind her own quieter nature, use it as an excuse?

"I begin to wonder if there are different paths for each of us and if I've wandered off the one designed for me. I don't know." A tear spilled over and trickled down her face. "I need to rediscover what my path is."

The shadows on his face revealed he either did not understand or did not like her answer. So be it. She'd not refute nor temper her words. It was time to choose. Return to what she knew would please her Lord, seeking—and obeying—His will. Or stay the comfortable path she'd carved for herself.

CHAPTER THIRTEEN

July

Syntyche promised herself she'd tell Tymon of Euodia's friendship with Malitta the next time she saw him. But the next time, he was with a group of merchants, and the time after that, he returned home in such a foul mood she feared he'd act rashly and be thrown in the same prison she'd been in. Then he was standing in the kitchen saying he was leaving for a business trip and "next time" moved further away.

She'd tell Euodia herself if they were speaking. Ignoring the sense that she should act, she squelched thoughts of Euodia betrayed or hurt. Malitta would not hurt little Euodia. Everyone loved her, and Euodia seemed to love everyone back. If she said a word against Malitta, Euodia would defend her, especially since last worship day when Syntyche had marched Malitta to a private corner of the churchyard. Had she been too harsh?

"Do not dare show your face at my home again or I will have you thrown outside. Ty told me how you betrayed his friend Marcus. And do not call me your friend. I am not. I do not trust you. You lied to me and used me. Stay away from my family."

Malitta had not run to Euodia, but Syntyche saw other women gathering around her. It was likely one of them told Euodia of the incident. Malitta, with her penchant for lying and casting blame on others, would warp the truth to persuade others she was unjustly accused.

It was better if Tymon dealt with it. If he believed their sister to be in danger, he'd warn Marcellus or insist Euodia no longer befriend the woman. Euodia half adored, half feared their big brother and would do as he advised without questioning or arguing.

"Next time" came without warning.

Clipping thyme from the garden, she jumped when his voice came from behind her.

"Synee. It's been a long time since Euodia and Marcellus have joined us for a meal. Why?"

She ignored his question. "Good day, Tymon. Did you have a good trip? Did you just return?"

"Yes. Why so long? Tell me."

She brushed away a bee and scooted to the rosemary. "Tell me, tell me, tell me. Have you forgotten the word 'please'?"

"Is it your monthly time?"

"Tymon!"

He rubbed a hand over his face. "Sorry. My steward heard a rumor—more than one—that I can hardly credit. First, tell me, *please,* is it true you and Euodia brawled in the street?"

"Brawled? No. Disagreed, yes."

"Loudly."

"There was a thunderstorm overhead. We raised our voices to hear each other."

"In public."

"It was a small street."

Kneeling before him as he towered above her, she felt like a naughty child. She stood, though her head still reached only to his shoulder.

He studied her until she looked away in discomfort. When he spoke, his words were flat. Unemotional.

"This is why I do not believe in your Jesus God. Never before your involvement with Him would you have caused a scene so ugly that it is repeated in the streets. You've always been too outspoken for a woman, but you've never embarrassed our family before this. You've become harsh, and Euodia has become more like you, not the kind and loving God you profess."

The thyme and rosemary in her hands fell unheeded to the ground.

He shook his head, bewilderment creasing his features. "Why would I ever want to be a follower of His?"

She fell back a step, gasped as his words slammed the breath from her lungs. She should have stayed kneeling. Of all the people she'd ever wanted to know the Lord, Tymon and Alex were most important to her. Alex died before he could hear of the Lord. Tymon rejected Him because of her.

"Tymon, no. Do not judge my Lord by me."

His eyebrow quirked. "How else can I judge Him? You expect me to trust when a stranger speaks truth about the change within? You are the one I know, the one I'd see a difference in."

Frantic, she clutched his arm. "You must know Him for yourself."

"Synee, watching you, I don't want to know Him." He patted her hand. "I do not say this in contempt or to shame you. Your faith holds no interest for me, and I've explained why."

"Oh, Ty..."

"Synee, you hold to your faith as you will. I do not forbid it if it brings you peace—though I see no peace in you. Losing the baby and Alex and then your business and house, those are hard things. You must take joy where you can. I hold to my faith in my abilities. Do not try to change me, and I will say nothing more of your faith."

He curled his hand around the back of his neck. "There is another matter—a rumor that horrifies me as much as or more than my sisters making a spectacle of themselves."

Syntyche dragged her focus back to him, away from berating herself for destroying any hope her brother would come to faith. Numbly she stared at him. What could he have heard that was worse?

"Malitta."

Her heart sank. She'd delayed telling him. Inwardly she cringed, imagining his fury when he realized she'd known and done nothing.

"Did you know Euodia associates with that woman? Calls her 'friend'?"

A squeaky "yes" emerged from her mouth. Clearing her throat, she tried again. "I intended to tell you."

"Before or after the damage was done?"

She quaked at the thunder on his face. Ty did not accept excuses.

"I-I haven't seen Euodia—that is, we haven't spoken, and I thought it would be better…maybe she'd listen to you."

"Not spoken after a public brawl. I see. So, after all I revealed to you, tell me—is the problem that you did not understand the harm Malitta is capable of causing, or that you cannot bring yourself to think of anyone other than yourself and your pride?"

The deadly softness of his voice unnerved her.

"I expected better of you even before this Jesus infatuation. Is this how your God teaches you to behave, to protect yourself but cower from protecting your own family? I'm going to the sister I love and warn her of the danger. Syntyche, if she's shed one tear because of that woman, it will not go well for you."

"I warned Malitta to stay away."

"Did you tell Euodia why? No? What do you think she will do when her 'friend' avoids her? Do you think she'll accept it, shrug her shoulders, and go merrily on her way? Can you think of nothing outside yourself?"

Disgust dripped from his words.

"Ty, I'm sorry. I didn't think…."

"You remind me of Malitta." He pivoted and stalked away.

Of Malitta?

She staggered beneath the sick feeling of no return, of being the cause of an irreparable rift. If Ty spoke truth, she could not bear it.

Dazed, she crumpled to the ground amid the bitter herbs and huddled in a ball, unable to stand beneath the weight of Ty's accusations. She lay without moving, without thinking, her face pressed against the strewn herbs, the scent of rosemary stinging her nose.

Around her, sunlit colors dimmed as twilight cast its gray tint across the garden. The whir of mosquito wings replaced the bees' buzz. A nightjar with its tiny beak and long tail feathers darted within reach. Somewhere far away she heard children squealing, maters calling, an early owl announcing his presence.

Flat toes appeared in her vision.

"Mistress, you sleep?"

By force of will, Syntyche gathered herself into an upright position.

The girl giggled. "Your skin has grown green."

She brushed the nettles and dirt from her face, feeling the indentations they'd made.

"Demi—that's your name, isn't it—has my brother returned?"

"No, and I'm glad. He looked scary angry when he left here." She stuck out her lower lip. "He frowned at me, but I didn't do anything to him. I just asked if he'd want dinner and…"

The girl chattered on about the injustice she suffered, and Syntyche's mind wandered. Neither had she done anything to offend him. The dissent was between sisters and the church. If Ty stayed out of it, and Malitta and Clement and everyone else left them alone and stopped meddling, maybe the misunderstanding between them could be resolved and they'd go back to their old relationship.

Ty had spoken in anger to hurt her and cover his own guilt. He had no right to take out his overprotectiveness of Euodia on her. Nor was Malitta her fault nor the quarrel while helping the mal aria patients. How dare he say she was like Malitta? Syntyche curled her fingers into her palms until the nails cut into skin. She was nothing like that woman.

She'd show them all. She'd continue witnessing, continue to use her confidence to tell other women about the Lord. No one could make her stop. No one could take this away from her.

It was all she had.

CHAPTER FOURTEEN

Euodia coiled her hair, pinned on her oldest stola, and scooped up Linus to deliver to the kitchen boy's care. Tapping the boy on his thin shoulder, she lifted a single finger to her lips. He nodded, accustomed to the routine of caring for the bundle of white fluff during Euodia's early-morning ventures into the city. She'd thank him with a coin or a sweetmeat. Once, she'd bought him new sandals. His missing-tooth smile was all the thanks she needed.

Having escaped both her assigned guard and Claudia, Euodia inhaled the freshness of the morning. Its lovely mildness would not last long. By midday, the city would be toasty warm and she'd have wilted. Serving others must be done early in the day. The earliness also kept her time from home less noticeable to Amelia.

Citing concerns for his villa, Atticus had left earlier this week. Amelia stayed. Was it forever? Every day her friends gathered to defame anyone absent and play card games, and she was expected to sit attentively, ready to meet their slightest need. These morning walks allowed her to stretch her legs, enjoy the outdoors, and continue to help the hurting.

Reaching the Via Egnatia, she turned toward the still-sleepy forum. Two of today's errands could be accomplished quickly at the center of town—anonymously paying taxes for Noah, a brother in Christ who had lost his job, and buying bay leaves to burn. The spice and floral scent might soothe the man's anxiety until he found another job. Maybe Marcellus needed another groom in the stable.

Considering how to approach Marcellus with the suggestion, Euodia noticed a furtive woman leaving the Egyptian temple. Something in the way the woman moved made her think of Valeria. Impossible, of course. Valeria worshiped Roman gods and refused to leave her bed until late morning. Besides, she was alone—unwise for a noble heiress.

The woman tripped and fell. Seeing she struggled to stand, Euodia hurried across the road.

"Let me help you up."

"Go away." The muffled voice sounded teary.

Euodia drew back, uncertain if she should walk away or stay until the woman regained her feet. As she debated, a light breeze feathered open the woman's veil.

Valeria? Hair mussed, robe soiled, face tear-streaked and splotchy? Yes, she recognized the embroidered purse Valeria clutched.

Valeria's red-rimmed eyes had widened in fear or dismay, Euodia wasn't sure which. Ignoring the objections, she slid her hands beneath Valeria's arms and lifted her to stand.

"Do not touch me. You do not want to touch me."

"Did I hurt you? Are you bruised? Injured?"

Valeria shook her head in mute denial. "Just go away."

"I'm going to see you home."

"No."

Euodia smiled to soften her words. "I'm more stubborn than you are, my friend."

Valeria covered her face and sobbed. "No one will ever call me that again. I am doomed to die alone, my name a curse. Forsaken and friendless."

Dramatic Valeria. "You have many friends who will never leave you." She curved her arm around Valeria's waist, refusing to release her when she stiffened. She coaxed her to move forward.

"What has you so upset? Tell me." Euodia suppressed a grin. She'd sounded like her brother with that impervious command.

Valeria said nothing until they reached the entrance to her magnificent home. "I will show you my fate. You will never speak to me nor see me again." Her eyes fixed on Euodia's, she drew up her sleeve to expose her skin.

Euodia gasped, but as Valeria hurriedly covered her arm and began to turn away, she reached out. Valeria stared at the hand touching her leprous arm.

"You wish to die with me?"

Show her.

The Lord's words from many months ago now made sense.

"Not in the least, my friend. I wish you to live. Will you allow me to look closer?"

"Why? To tell of my ugliness to others?"

"Valeria, before I married Marcellus, I learned about herbs and treatments so I could ease my pater's stomach pains and my mater's aches. I still work among the poor who cannot afford a physician. I have some knowledge, some skills. What you share with me remains between us."

Valeria's attempt at ridicule emerged as pathos. "You help? I have entreated the Roman gods, the Egyptian gods, the Greek gods. None have healed me, and you think you can?"

Lord?

Show her.

Without those words, she'd have backed away at Valeria's challenge.

"I think you are desperate enough to let me try. May I?"

"You fool! There is no cure."

Euodia dipped her head in acknowledgement of that truth. "If it is leprosy, there is no cure. If it is not, there are ways to manage the pain and disguise the marks." She swallowed so loudly it was impossible Valeria didn't hear her. "I serve a different God, and He has told me to help you. May I?"

"Why would your God help me? Why is He punishing you with living death?" She curled her arms protectively over her body. "It's absurd. I don't even know His name or at which temple you offer sacrifices to plead for favor."

"I worship the Almighty and His Son, the Lord Jesus. I join with other believers to worship Him, but we offer only the sacrifice of listening and obeying as He leads. He has told me to help you because He loves you."

"Then He's blind. I'm ugly now. Hideous."

"You are loved as you are. That is why He sent me to you today, to show you this truth."

Eyes tender, she allowed Valeria to search her face for deception or assurance. Whatever Valeria saw disarmed her.

She lowered the mask of haughtiness, and entreaty poured from the leprous woman. "If...maybe you can help. I don't know where else to turn, but if there is a possibility your God knows... If you are not afraid..."

"I am not afraid." Much. "Let's go to your room so I can look closer and ask more questions."

In past visits, Euodia had tarried in the entrance and atrium to marvel at the cool beauty of Valeria's home, the silver-white curtains, the white and gold cushions. Today, she glanced with little interest at the ornate furnishings and exquisite artwork and hurried past them to keep up with her friend.

Once they were in a private room with all servants dismissed and the door locked, Valeria bared her arm. Euodia studied the white splotches.

"Squeeze my hand as hard as you can. Good." Euodia prodded both elbows and felt Valeria's neck. She smiled at her friend. "Your elbows and neck are not swollen. Your grip is strong." She scraped the pale patches of skin with her fingernail and was rewarded with a wince and scowl.

"Are there other places your skin lost color or feeling? No? Valeria, I do not know what caused your skin to fade, but you are not showing the signs of leprosy. You have strength in your grip and feeling where the whiteness has spread."

"Not leprosy?" Hope bloomed in her voice. "Will it go away?" She touched her face. "Will it spread? Will everyone know?"

"I think the whiteness will remain for a few weeks, maybe a month or two, but not spread. It most often appears on the face or hands and elbows. Be thankful it is your arm and can be hidden beneath your clothes. From my experience in healing, I'm confident that if you are careful, no one will know." Pleased with the good news, she waited for Valeria's effusive appreciation and admiration of her knowledge.

Valeria pursed her mouth. "If you and your God know this is not leprosy—you are sure? There is no doubt, it is not leprosy?"

"Trust me."

She slitted her eyes. "Then the priests also knew. They lied to me. I paid outrageous amounts for their silence. They lied to me."

Pacing back and forth, she quickened her steps, her words short and rapid.

"Trust. Who? Not priests. Not my god. Liars, all." She whirled, pointed at Euodia. "Maybe you lie as well. You and your God. My skin might be rotting, and you deceive me in retaliation for some imagined offense." She threw the heavily embroidered pouch at Euodia's feet. "Take this to your God and go. I've dealt with people like you. If I hear a word of this, your family will regret they ever knew your name."

Euodia picked up the pouch and walked to the door. "In a few weeks, you will know who lies and who speaks truth. Then you will trust me."

Shoulders drooping, she left the house, its beauty tarnished by the vitriol it held. She'd seen Valeria's reaction in others when someone regretted sharing a secret or revealing shame.

Rather than expressing gratitude for acceptance or easing of suffering, she was shoved away with false accusations, the person's embarrassment in being vulnerable disguised as anger.

Why had she imagined a woman as proud and self-centered as Valeria might be different?

Her morning almost gone, she walked quickly to the tax office to pay Noah's overdue taxes. The bay leaves must wait. She'd send the purse of coins to Brother Clement to distribute as he thought best. By now, Amelia would be awake and demanding her presence.

Claudia met Euodia at the door, the servant's eyes giving silent warning of Amelia's displeasure with the unexplained absence. It seemed no one was happy with her these days.

A sigh escaped her. She wasn't too happy with herself either. Yes, she'd obeyed the Lord's guidance to show Valeria unconditional acceptance, but instead of pointing to Him, she'd pointed to herself.

Her feet dragged despite Claudia's urging her to the dining room where Amelia waited. Euodia coughed as waves of incense assailed her nostrils and clogged her throat.

Amelia's lip curled in contempt. "You represent our name and noble house, yet you walk the streets looking"—her eyes raked Euodia—"like that."

"I'm sorry, Mater."

Amelia shuddered. "To be called mater by a mere merchant's daughter. Do not disgrace the title again."

"I meant to return much sooner, but a friend invited me to her home."

"A peasant friend, no doubt. Who of any importance would lower herself to be seen with you when you look little better than a servant?"

Euodia bristled. "Valeria Marcus Dominus. You met her at Juno's banquet." Valeria, a distant cousin of Nero, was a name Amelia would approve of for her daughter-in-law. That should stop her criticism. "We had not visited in a while, so when she invited me, I accepted."

"Valeria?" Color drained from Amelia's face. "You went in her home?"

"Yes."

Amelia bolted to her feet. "You fool. Not an hour ago, I heard she has leprosy." Eyes bulging, she screeched, "You've brought living death into my house!"

"My house."

Either Amelia did not hear or chose to ignore her. "Order my carpentum. Now!"

"Valeria does not have leprosy. I have seen her skin. Touched it."

Amelia's scream pierced the air. "Touched it! You touched it? Stay away from me!" Shoving slaves from her path and careening around flaming braziers, she lunged for the door, toppling the busts of her ancestors from their pedestals and tripping over her feet.

Euodia followed, hands outstretched. "Amelia, think! If it was leprosy, the priests would exile her, not accept bribes for their silence, not even with her connections to Caesar. They'd not risk being disfigured and dying in a cave for a handful of coins."

Amelia paused in the doorway to sneer. "You ignorant, presumptuous fool. Juno's priests have declared it is leprosy. It is so."

Within a quarter of an hour, Amelia scrambled into the carriage to return to her villa. In the ensuing chaos, the remaining servants and slaves tossed bedding, art, clothes, and books into hastily retrieved crates. Carts were requisitioned for transportation, furniture disassembled, rugs sloppily rolled and thrust on top of delicate silver pitchers and trays.

The last cart careened away, leaving two mismatched pillow tassels, piles of crumpled parchment, a stray shoe, and an overturned bench. A forgotten basket, food scraps, and hairpins littered the entrance. The outside door stood ajar, revealing a broken table discarded in the street.

Studiously, Euodia avoided the eyes of her servants, uncertain what her face might communicate. Relief? Anger? Dismay?

Would Marcellus understand? In helping Valeria, did she forever forfeit a pleasant relationship with Amelia? If Amelia knew of Valeria's "leprosy," others did too. Would Valeria accuse her of breaking a confidence?

A strange, long silence penetrated her thoughts. Her people waited, their tension palpable as if they hoped for reassurance.

"Valeria does not have leprosy. I have not brought it into our home. You are safe."

No one spoke.

Lord?

In answer, her stomach growled.

"Doris, tell Cook the kitchen is again hers, and we are hungry."

Relief sighed among them. With evidence of her continued presence and a normal request, they dared believe she spoke truth.

"Felix, hire help to bring our things from storage. Anna, see that the guest rooms are cleaned. Claudia, you and I will set things right in here. Bring cleaning supplies. Doris, send this purse to Clement. Tell him it is a gift for the church but not from me."

As the servants scattered to obey her directions, Euodia traced the Lord's hand in this morning's events. So long ago, He'd sparked an interest in medicine, taught her the difference between leprosy and the skin whitening, and given her the courage not to shy away at Valeria's first refusal of help. Today, He'd crossed their paths, allowing comfort for Valeria, and then removed Amelia from her home.

How else did He move, unseen, in her life? In a few days, she'd attend worship and give thanks for His guidance.

"Mistress, you have a guest—a man. I do not recognize him but allowed him to wait in the atrium. Did I do right? He's very tall. Do you want a guard close by?"

Euodia hid a smile at the girl's earnest desire to please. She'd bought, freed, and hired her a week ago. Little Tira took her new life and responsibilities very seriously.

"You did well. Did he give a name?"

"Yes, mistress. Tymon."

"Tira, that's my brother. I'm pleased you did not send him on his way. Here, take Linus, and I will see to my guest."

Euodia checked herself in the mirror, patted her hair, and slipped on her house shoes before hurrying to the atrium.

She held out both hands in welcome. "Tymon, I'm glad you are here. It is such a pleasure to see you."

His taut face dimmed her smile.

Heart thudding, she tensed. "Ty, is all well?"

A brief smile cracked his solemn demeanor. "Forgive me, Sister. I bring no tidings of illness or injury. I am well as is our sister and, as far as I know, your husband."

"Yet you are troubled. Come, walk with me in the garden and share what concerns you. We will be alone, and you can speak openly."

Euodia led them through the rose-lined path to a bench halfway down the garden. She sat and patted the seat beside her. "As you like to say, tell me."

"You will not like what I have to tell you." He sat heavily. "First, do you trust me?"

"Completely."

"Do you believe I care for you and will always protect you?"

"Yes. You're frightening me. What is this about, Ty?"

"I warned Synee and thought she'd warn you—never mind. That's another conversation. There is a person in your life, one you call friend, whom I have known for many years. She is not a true friend to anyone. Her words cannot be trusted."

"Malitta."

Astonishment jumped across his face. "You know?"

"I suspected."

His amazement so comical, she laughed. "Ty, I notice things about people—their eyes shifting or darkening, their hands clenching the way yours are now, the set of their shoulders, and the tone of their voices. The more I watched her and considered her words and actions, the more I realized she is deceptive. I cannot point to one incident or mannerism, but pooled together, I know." She frowned. "And I think I remember her."

"You were very young."

"And small enough to hide beneath the sofa."

Disbelief contorted his face. Then a breath of relief whooshed out. "You understand my concern?"

"I do."

"And you will stop associating with her?"

"No."

"No? By all the stars in the sky, why not?"

Euodia nibbled her lower lip then grinned. "You will not like what I have to tell you."

Tymon snorted.

"My Lord Jesus says all are worthy of salvation and forgiveness. I cannot walk away from her because she is not perfect." She grinned. "I'm not perfect either, but don't tell anyone."

Unsmiling, he dragged his hand down his face. "Another Jesus thing. Euodia, I'm not speaking of perfection. I'm speaking of dangerous."

"Will she hurt me, stab me?"

"Not with a blade. Her knives are well-honed words and a well-hidden snare of betrayal."

"I will not walk away from Malitta. Someday she may be my sister in the Lord. I must befriend her, show her a different way, try to get along with her."

Tymon stood. Disdain swept across his countenance. "You won't walk away from Malitta, but you can walk away from Syntyche? Try getting along with your own sister before you talk to me of your Lord." Back stiff, he trudged away, leaving her sitting on the bench open-mouthed.

A deep buzzing rang in her ears. Heartsick at the truth Ty spoke, she sat motionless, her stomach churning. Linus whimpered and nudged her toes. She could not summon the strength to pet him. Or to cry. Or to speak.

Torrents of hurt flooded her, hurts too deep to name, too shameful to voice. If she could not maintain a relationship with her sister, or live as a believer before her brother, who was she to teach others of the Lord Christ?

Or even call herself a Christ follower? Saved, forgiven, yes. But one who seeks to be like Christ? Cheeks flaming at the failure, she pressed icy hands to her face to cool its heat.

Longing for escape from her misery, she thought only of crawling in bed. Maybe when she woke she'd discover this had all been a bad dream. Deeply troubled, she turned inward, shunning the One whose comfort and guidance waited her call.

CHAPTER FIFTEEN

August

"Forgive us our debts as we forgive others...."

The familiar words wrenched Syntyche's prayer to a standstill. The others gathered in the small building continued to voice the Lord's Prayer. She did not.

Forgive? No. Walls of rebellion and refusal closed in, invisible but as impenetrable as those that had imprisoned her for a week with poor Hagne.

Forgive others? Not until they asked. Not Clement or Malitta or Euodia. Not those who scorned her at worship. Not the guard who struck her. Not Albus nor his crone of a daughter, Mania. Not Tymon and his failure to believe in her.

No one realized how much she'd suffered. No one stepped forward to make amends to her. No one understood the ache she woke to each day, grieving her husband and child, longing for a place to call her own. Nevertheless, she'd not swim in a river of pity tears. She'd keep giving and giving.

"...giving thanks and making amends. An opportunity we need." Clement's voice broke her thoughts. "It is a Jewish celebration I would like to adapt to our needs and observe this year. You know I am Roman and Syzygus is a Philippian, so I have asked our Jewish brother, Aaron, to tell us more about Rosh Hoshanah, which begins at the next new moon. Brother?"

Aaron, a frail man with a booming voice, stepped forward. "Rosh Hoshanah is the Jewish new year. For two days there is rejoicing and celebration and food." An ethereal smile crinkled the lines around his deep, age-set eyes. "Oh, the food. So much food. Delicious food. Food you dream of for days to come."

The rumbling chuckle shook his whole body. "I look small, but I can eat!"

The congregation laughed as he patted his stomach. Syntyche nodded with the others. She'd seen Aaron eat more than a man twice his size.

He slapped his forehead. "I'm thinking of food and forgot. Rosh Hoshanah is also the time we believe the Almighty created the world—a birthday celebration of creation."

He beamed. "Birthday food is very good."

Aaron shook his finger at the congregation. "Ahh, but after those two days of magnificent meals when you eat more than you thought possible, there are ten days of reflection and repentance."

Syntyche caught herself grinning as another of Aaron's chuckles rolled out.

"Not because of all you ate—the beautiful, braided *challah* with mounds of soft warmness and the pomegranate honey chicken and the *tzimmes* and the saffron rice with raisins and the couscous with seven vegetables and the apples and honey and the..." He wiped the corner of his lips and grinned wryly. "You see, my mouth waters at the thought."

Aaron squinted. "Where was I before the food? Ten days, yes. These ten days are called the Days of Awe."

His bony shoulders drew up in a shrug. "Why, you ask? Very well, I will tell you. Because of the awesome burden we Jews feel to atone for our misdeeds, the awesome desire to make peace with others before we face God's judgment on Yom Kippur." He chortled and slapped his knee. "You heard Days of Awe and thought there would be ten more days of fasting with incredible food, yes? No.

"It is a time of asking for forgiveness from those you've wronged, whether it is through gossip or cheating or..." He chuckled and shook his finger at the boys on the front row. "...even throwing your apple core into someone's courtyard."

He surveyed the people before him. "It is also a time for considering how you have sinned against the Lord."

His deep voice dropped. "At the end of the ten days, there is Yom Kippur, the Day of Atonement. It is a solemn day when we confess our sins and those of our community to the Almighty and plead for His forgiveness. We fast for twenty-five hours to show our contrition, our sincerity of remorse, and to focus on our relationship with our Creator."

"And then?"

Syntyche did not recognize the voice from the men's section.

"And then we go back to living life. It is a new year, a fresh beginning, a time we have not yet soiled with selfishness."

Brother Clement stood to move forward. Aaron stopped him with an upheld hand.

"Please, grant me another minute. There is more you must know to understand my people better." Sadness stole across his face, his voice pensive. "To those not yet believers in our Lord Jesus, not resting in His assurance of eternal life, this is a most serious occasion. The ten days are to repent and make sure your name is sealed in the Book of Life and not the Book of Death—a time you try to change God's mind if you are in the wrong book. Each year my people face Yom Kippur—Judgment Day. Each year they must work to be written and sealed in the Book of Life. They do not have the peace we share."

Clement grasped Aaron's shoulder. "Thank you, Brother."

"But I have not told you about the shofar or casting bread on waters."

"We will hear from you again." Clement addressed the congregation. "It is obvious to Brother Syzygus and me that our church needs a time of healing. Therefore, we will feast on the day of Rosh Hoshanah not as a new year but to pray for a new beginning. We will reflect privately during the ten Days of Awe. Let this be a time of reconciliation, a time to heal the broken relationships among us and between us and nonbelievers."

Clement gestured toward Aaron and Syzygus. "After much discussion, we will not observe Yom Kippur. As believers, Jesus is the atonement for our sins, and we are already sealed in the Book of Life. Instead, we will gather for a second feast to commence a new beginning for our church and to prepare for our Lord's arrival. We do not know the exact day of His return, but He has commanded us to watch and be ready for our King and Savior."

He smiled toward Aaron. "I suspect the second feast will be more magnificent than the first."

Aaron clasped his hands together and bowed. "So be it." He looked up and grinned. "I will take care to prepare myself."

Above the people's laughter, Clement interjected, "Whoever feels led to help prepare the feasts, speak with me before you leave today."

Syntyche saw him search for her as he spoke. She'd make it easy for him to apologize by offering to lead the preparation for the feasting. His contrition and stammering words might melt her heart. She'd hesitate as if considering his apology and then let her feelings for him…

Alex's face appeared in her mind. Feelings for Clement? He could not replace her Alex, and yet she wanted to spend time with Clement, have his golden eyes light up like the sun when she entered a room, see his wide smile.

Most everyone had begun their journey back to the city when she approached Clement. He watched her advance, unaware her heart thumped against her chest with each step she took.

Standing before him, she searched for his blush, the lowered eyes of regret, the awkwardness fronting his apology. Uneasy heat rose in her face. She glanced away and back again.

His gaze remained steady, his manner neither welcoming nor forbidding—exactly as she would have comported herself had he come to her. She faltered. If he thought she meant to apologize to him, he was mistaken.

"Sister Syntyche."

She waited for him to continue. Silence swelled to discomfort.

"The feast. I am willing… I want… I can direct preparations for the feast. Both. Both the feasts. The first and the second. Feasts." Snapping her mouth shut, she fumed, embarrassed by the stumbling offer of her well-known cooking skills. He should have come to her and requested she lead the preparations.

"Good. We will meet with the others tomorrow in my home to decide how to proceed. Excuse me, I must speak with someone else."

She stared at his back. Those broad shoulders had not hunched in shame. No tears glistened or even glimmered in his dark-lashed eyes. The stutters and stammers—hers, not his.

Bewildered, she began the trek to the city.

CHAPTER SIXTEEN

Syntyche's brisk steps faltered. Euodia's single-horse carriage stood outside Clement's house. Coincidence? Or was her sister one of the "others" he'd mentioned yesterday? Slowly she approached the entrance and knocked. Since the girl who opened the door was new and didn't know her, Syntyche didn't ask who else was present.

Led past the atrium into Clement's office, she braced herself for a flurry of apologies, not for the light fading from Euodia's face as she turned toward her.

"Syntyche." Clement and Euodia spoke as one.

"Euodia, Brother Clement." Syntyche dipped her head graciously.

No other words broke the silence until Clement cleared his throat. "A benefactor has provided the funds for us to purchase whatever is needed for our feasts. My kitchen is available—"

"And mine, since my in-laws have left."

"Mine, also. Brother, how many others will be joining us?"

The lines surrounding Clement's eyes tightened. "None. They withdrew upon learning you and Euodia would be involved."

Euodia's quick intake of breath told Syntyche her sister was as surprised as she was. "Why? We are both known to be excellent cooks, although Euodia spends less time in the kitchens since her marriage. Our efforts will not embarrass anyone."

Steadily, Clement met her defiance. "It is not your cooking that embarrasses."

Syntyche hated the heat staining her face.

"I am trying to persuade a few of the women to work together so you two do not bear the entire burden, but all have refused to work alongside either of you. They do not want to choose sides, nor feel they are being coerced to choose."

In the deadening silence, a servant slipped into the room and spoke in a soft voice to Clement.

"Our meeting must be cut short. A messenger has come, one I've been expecting for a long time. I must speak with him immediately." Something indecipherable flashed in his eyes. "I expect to see you both at worship."

Euodia avoided looking at anyone as she left Clement's house. She climbed into the carriage, directing it home instead of to the visits she'd planned.

Questions raced through her thoughts. How much had the servant girl heard, and what had she told the other servants? Had her carriage driver smirked at her? Had Clement confided in Helena that others refused to work alongside her and Syntyche? Who else knew of this?

At least Lydia's work required her to return to Phoenicia. Maybe by the time she completed her travels, all this would be forgotten and never mentioned. If Paul ever heard...Euodia recoiled from completing the thought.

Was she an object of gossip and rumors? She clapped a hand over her mouth in dismay. Was it possible a patient might refuse her help because rumors of her disgrace reached their ears?

If Marcellus ever heard of this... She'd been so excited sharing Marcellus's decision with Clement, and all that time he'd been listening, he'd known the other women wanted nothing to do with her and Syntyche. At least Clement couldn't know of Tymon's reprimand. She shuddered. That would be too much to bear. Would Clement have revealed that others refused to work with them if Syntyche hadn't asked?

Worship service was in six days. Would her face still be burning? How could she look the other women in the eye? If Clement hadn't spoken forcibly about them attending, she'd plead illness.

Frustrated with questions that had no answers, she crossed her legs, and her foot begin to jiggle. Why would they not be willing to work with her? She was not the abrasive one. She was the one most people felt at ease with confiding their sorrows, knowing her words would bring comfort. Was she no longer trusted?

Home, she gathered Linus in her arms to scratch his chin. She refused Claudia's offer of food, her stomach in knots, her entire being unsettled. The expression in Clement's eyes when he admonished them to be at worship seemed more of a command, as if he surmised something she did not want to know.

Frowning in concentration, she could not untangle what she sensed was knotted.

If Marcellus were home, she could confide in him about... No, maybe not. The other women's pettiness toward her was a poor reflection of believers. It was good he was away. By the time he returned home, maybe everything would be settled.

Feeling lonely, she wished she had someone to talk to, to help her sort her thoughts and feelings. Someone who'd find the absurd and help her laugh. Someone who'd hug her and let her cry but not too long. Someone like a sister.

The day of worship gifted the world with a brilliantly blue sky. Syntyche had hoped for rain or a flood or an earthquake—a little one—just enough to keep everyone home.

She dressed with her usual indifference, proof to everyone she was not upset or concerned with the opinions of others. In the kitchen, she reached for the largest, sharpest knife. With a single swipe, she cleaved the bread loaf in half. It was efficient. She was not at all anxious.

In spite of her efforts to be late, she left at the usual time. Attempting to stall her arrival—only because it was hard to sit for long-winded Syzygus's teachings—she shortened her stride and minced steps as she'd seen some of the noble elite do, but the walk to worship passed quickly.

No one other than Helena called greetings to her in the courtyard. Odd. Until a few weeks ago, women and children had gravitated toward her, vying for her attention. Disgruntled, she entered the building to wait until time for the service. Euodia sat a couple of rows away with Malitta, both their heads bowed. Syntyche slouched in her seat wondering whether they bowed in remorse or prayer.

From outside came surges of laughter and joyful greetings as if a dear friend was being welcomed home from a long journey. Who had been away? The only person she could think of was Epaphroditus. She bolted upright. He must be the messenger Clement spoke of two days ago. Epaphroditus would have a message from Paul!

With a deep sigh of relief, her spirits lifted. She would be vindicated, Euodia chastened. The ones who'd ignored her earlier this morning would regret their actions. She should have taken more care with her appearance since she'd be observed as she forgave Euodia and hugged her as only a sister could hug.

With her next breath, dread replaced relief. Her precious sister would be devastated when Clement called her aside and spoke to her after the service. The poor girl had no idea what was about to happen. Determined to protect Euodia, she vowed to stand beside her, comforting and encouraging her in the wake of Paul's correction.

The believers crowded in. Clement stopped and regarded her, his beautiful eyes sorrowful. Instead of reassuring her that he'd finally recognized his fault, they spread the cold fingers of apprehension along her spine.

Shuffling to the front of the believers, Brother Syzygus leaned on Epaphroditus's arm. "Brothers and sisters, today we rejoice in our brother's return from Rome. We shared with you that he'd fallen ill on his return journey but did not realize he almost died—"

He waited until the gasps and comments quieted. "But after five months, he has come home safely and with a letter to our church from our brother Paul. After our songs and prayers of thanksgiving, Brother Clement will read it aloud."

Praise filled the church as the believers joined in prayer and thanksgiving until Clement motioned for them to be seated. When quiet prevailed, he unrolled the scroll and began.

"To all God's holy people in Christ Jesus at Philippi, together with the overseers and deacons: Grace and peace to you from God our Father and the Lord Jesus Christ..."

The words rolled over her, filling her with joy, reminding her of the hope she had in Christ. As Clement continued reading, she wept to think of her dear friend Paul in chains, and nodded when he mentioned suffering—together they had suffered here in Philippi, working alongside each other to tell others of the Lord.

"Do everything without grumbling...."

She knew a few people who needed to hear that. Twisting to see if they were here, she nodded. They looked shamefaced. Good.

"Forgetting what is behind and straining toward what is ahead..."

She'd heard Paul say that before when people protested their sins were too great for forgiveness or when they slid back into sin and sought to repent.

"Therefore, my brothers and sisters...my joy and crown...dear friends."

Yes, she was Paul's sister in the Lord, her work one of his joys, his dear friend.

"I plead with Euodia..."

She gasped. No! Cease! Not like this! Quick! Inhale the words before they are heard. Stumble, say you misread it. Paul wrote this? Their beloved friend Paul rebuked her sister by name? In the presence of everyone she knew? To all the churches who would receive copies of the letter? She cringed, unable to bear that Euodia's shame was blatantly proclaimed.

"...and I plead with Syntyche..."

Her world stopped—breath, motion, thought. Her eyes riveted on Clement.

"...to be of the same mind in the Lord..."

"Yes, and I ask you, my true companion—" Clement paused and nodded to Syzygus. "That's you, faithful one, and as your very name proclaims—true yokefellow."

"...help these women..."

Both of them, singled out for correction in front of everyone? Clement continued reading. Syntyche stopped listening.

The reverberation clanging in her ears obliterated all other sound, all thought, all emotion. Be of the same mind. Of the same mind. The same mind. Be of the same mind. Same mind. A plea, a lament, an endless echo. If it did not stop, she'd rip the hair from her head.

Vaguely she realized people slipped past her as they left the building. Gradually she became aware someone was sobbing. Her movements stiff and slow, she turned toward the sound.

Euodia sat doubled over, her head cradled on Malitta's knees. Malitta glanced at her. Sneered.

Clement, with shoulders slumped, waited nearby with a solemn Syzygus. Both appeared as worn as if they had been the ones Paul corrected. Syzygus stood angled toward Euodia, but Clement, grief written on his face, his eyes bright with unshed tears, watched her.

Syntyche lurched to her feet, turned her back to them, and staggered from the building. She shook off a hand that grasped at her shoulder and pressed past someone who tried to stand in her path. Escape was all that mattered—from Euodia, from Clement, from scorn and reproach, from the Lord.

From herself.

CHAPTER SEVENTEEN

Syntyche walked through the city gates. She walked the stretch of the Via Egnatia within the city and out the gate leading to Thessalonika. If someone greeted her, she did not hear them. If someone waved or motioned her to join them, she did not see them. She did not weep nor hunger nor thirst. She walked resolutely, lifting one foot after another, continuing to move.

She moved forward relentlessly, ignoring the blisters that formed and broke, pushing herself to continue despite the scrapes of her ankles against rocks. She did not shy from the coiled snake nor slap at the mosquitoes feeding on her flesh. She slipped and fell on a downward slope, stood and trudged over the next ridge. She walked until she could no longer ignore the protest of her swollen, bleeding feet and was forced to rest by a large rock.

She braced for the onslaught of memories she'd known would happen as soon as she quit moving—Euodia's heart-rending sobs and Paul's plea battering her ears. Besieged by their echoes, today would scar and haunt her forever.

The flash of scorn from Malitta stung. So did the disappointment on Clement's sorrowful countenance. Both unexpected, unwarranted.

The sun, which must have been overhead when she left church, had dropped low enough that its sharp rays jabbed her eyes until they watered, the burning drops sliding down her face to nestle in the corners of her lips.

It would be dark soon, the night cool, but she did not turn toward home. She'd sit here, sleep if possible. Maybe morning would bring understanding, a solution, a comfort. She wrapped her arms around herself pretending Mater wrapped her in the soft blanket she'd woven.

Euodia wept until there were no tears, only dry gasps for air. Finally, she pushed herself upright, stared through swollen eyes at her tearstains on Malitta's lavender silk stola.

"I'm so sorry." She could hardly hear her own whisper.

Malitta's bracelets jangled as she brushed the silk. "I never liked this stola."

Euodia's eyes moistened at the kindness. Her attempt to smile a thank-you ended in another sob.

Malitta gathered her close. "I sent Syzygus and Clement on their way. Men seldom understand how deeply women hurt. I promised I'd see you home." She patted Euodia's back. "Everyone has left. Are you ready to leave?"

Euodia nodded but swayed when she stood.

"I knew I should have driven here today. We'll go as slowly as you need to and hire the first carriage we see in the city."

"Everyone left?" Euodia shifted to see where her sister had sat. "Everyone?"

"I didn't."

Another tear threatened. "Thank you, friend." She stumbled.

Malitta steadied her then wrapped an arm around her waist. "I cannot carry you, so don't twist your ankle."

Tentatively, Euodia started forward, one hand clinging to Malitta, the other hand holding her head to keep it from splintering into a hundred pieces. She concentrated on balancing. She hunched over the knots in her stomach, her legs wobbling with each step. Her grandparents had walked like this, each movement an effort, a triumph.

She'd never known one could grow old in a single minute.

Syntyche sifted through the words Paul had written until the rapid clopping of a horse penetrated the clatter of her thoughts. The hooves slowed, stopped. Iron-clad wheels creaked. She did not look up or move.

"Synee."

Tymon's voice sounded so far away.

"What were you thinking, being outside the city so late? Thank the gods, I found you."

Which God? No sound emerged.

"Your friend came to me—worried—said you'd been seen walking through the city and out the gates."

Which friend? Words refused to surface.

Tymon's shadow blocked the sun. Blessed relief. "Synee, can you hear me? Look at me."

Too much effort. She closed her eyes against his request.

A flask pressed her lips. She swallowed, licked her lips, swallowed again.

Tymon lifted her, carried her, positioned her in the carriage. She slumped against the cushions and slept, not waking until he settled her on her bed and untied her broken sandals. She whimpered as he pulled them from the crusted blood on her feet.

"You're going to be terribly sore tomorrow, little sister." He covered her with their mater's blanket.

She was sore now. Her head pounded. Her stomach cramped. Her legs and feet throbbed.

Her heart—ached.

Euodia woke to darkness. If only it could stay nighttime forever and she could stay pillowed in its safety. No one to see her or prod her with questions or expect anything of her. In the dark, her shame was invisible. Since others slept, her cries would go unheard, her anguish unnoticed. Closing her eyes, she sought a return to sleep, to escape.

It evaded her.

Instead, Paul's message pounded again and again—an inescapable lament—through the throbbing in her head. *"Be of one mind."*

Confusion piled atop humiliation and refused to leave. How? How could they be of the same mind when they were not? She'd never be as forthright as Syntyche nor Syntyche content to serve quietly.

Was she right and her sister wrong or vice versa? The knots in her stomach tightened. Paul requested the impossible with no instruction, no explanation of how to achieve it leaving them to flounder for understanding. It was beyond cruel. She'd considered Paul a friend, a brother in Christ as true as Syntyche was both her sister and friend and sister in Christ.

Tears soaked her temples. She was wrong on both accounts. Would a true friend humiliate her? Would a true sister judge without mercy?

"Lord, I feel so alone."

I am with you.

Realization dawned, cutting short the comfort of His presence. He'd been with her. She'd not been with Him. She'd ceased to rely on Him.

"Forgive me, Lord. Please, tell me what to do. I'm listening."

Joy.

She almost laughed. There could be no joy in this ordeal. The Lord spoke of an impossibility as ludicrous as Paul instructing her to be of one mind with her sister.

Remember.

She did remember. The last time she'd heard the word *joy,* Marcellus came to faith. Yes, God did the unlikely, but would He do it again?

She rubbed her head against its constant throbbing, against the intrusive doubt.

"Lord, just make it go away. I'll serve You every minute. I'll spend every coin Marcellus gives me on helping the poor. I'll obey Your every command. I'll stand in the forum and tell everyone about You, just make this go away."

Joy.

"No."

Silence filled the room.

"Do You hear me? I cannot find joy in this nightmare. It is too much to ask of me."

A shaft of light pierced her tender eyes. Claudia stood framed in the doorway, a lamp in her hand.

"Mistress? Did you call me or are you speaking to yourself?"

"No one." She dragged out cumbersome words. "I'm speaking to no one."

Syntyche woke herself up groaning. Turning over, she stretched and moaned. Tymon was not a prophet, but he'd accurately foretold how she'd feel this morning. Why did every part of her body hurt? Had she fallen from a horse? What had she done to be so—

Yesterday's travesty struck forcibly, its pain and shame kindling anger. How dare Paul include her as one to be "helped"? How dare Clement read her name aloud? If he cared for her at all, he'd have warned her or omitted those words or at least spoken them privately. No, he'd proclaimed them to the entire group of believers.

She shoved the bedcover away and edged her legs to the side of the bed. When the soles of her feet touched the floor, she cried out and fell backward. The pain lessened. Sitting up, she examined her feet. Blisters that had formed, broken and blistered again, still bled or oozed.

A knock sounded at the door.

"Mistress, did you call for me?"

"No. Yes. Tell me your name again. I've seen you in the kitchen."

"Demi." The curly head bobbed.

"Demi, light this lamp then hand me clean clothes. Is there warm water in the kitchen? Bring a basin and a cloth. Then heat more water and add salt to it. When it's ready, tell me." She sounded like Ty. "Please."

The girl returned with the basin and two cloths. "One for washing, one for drying. Do you need help, mistress?"

A sharp intake of breath told her Demi had seen the sores.

"That must hurt so much. How can I help you?"

Syntyche's eyes moistened. The girl's gentle spirit reminded her of Euodia, who would have been devastated by Paul's admonition. Her sister must be in as much pain as she was.

Somehow, they had to find their way back to each other. She had no idea how to start.

"The warm salt water will help, Demi. Bring it as soon as you can. It should be a little too hot since it will cool quickly."

Syntyche hobbled to the basin. Washed and dressed, she began to untangle her hair. The door squeaked and Demi entered, her tongue caught between her teeth as she balanced the full basin of swaying water. The girl positioned it by Syntyche's feet then moved behind her and took the brush from her hands.

"You soak your feet. I'll brush out the snarls."

Demi was a bit bossy, also like Euodia.

The salt stung. Syntyche jerked her feet out. Gritting her teeth, she dipped them in again, slowly. She had no choice if she wanted to avoid infection.

Demi's long brush strokes soothed, even as a thousand salty needles pricked the raw blisters of Syntyche's feet. She did not remove her feet again until the water cooled. When Demi brought more water, she clenched her jaw and repeated the process. Excruciating, it must be endured to prevent the infection from poisoning both feet or even both legs. She gagged remembering Euodia bandaging the stump of a man who'd lost his arm to an infected wound.

Infection. A thought grew like yeast in flour, and no matter how she punched it down it swelled again.

Infection had spread in the bond with her sister. Something had rubbed raw and wrong until a blister formed. Maybe neither of them recognized it. With no awareness or change between them, the blister burst, grew larger, burst again until all that could be seen was a sickly green, pus-filled wound.

It made sense. She'd felt the wrongness. But what had caused the blister? How did it begin?

Was Euodia gone from her forever? Fear puckered her mouth, sour like an unripe grape. Losing Euodia was like the gaping wound of losing another child. She'd been Euodia's mater and sister and best friend since the child was ten.

The next morning, Euodia squinted through swollen eyes as Claudia lit the braziers in her room and laid out fresh clothes.

"A woman came to see you two days ago. Said her name was Helena and you knew her, and she needed to talk with you. I told her you were not seeing anyone, but she insisted it was urgent."

"What?"

"A woman—"

"I heard that part. Two days ago?"

"Mistress, you've been asleep for three days."

Euodia rubbed grit from her eyes.

"If you hadn't awakened today, Cook and I would have sent for your sister."

"Claudia, do not send for anyone. Promise me. Don't permit anyone in the house either. I wish to be alone. Understand?"

"Yes."

The door opened, and three maids paraded in—each carrying a large bucket of steaming water. Behind them, Felix dragged in a tub.

Claudia stood with her hands on her hips. "You have neither eaten nor bathed in three days. I don't know what is wrong, if you are sick or upset, but a bath and food will help you feel better. After you've bathed and eaten, I'll leave you alone."

She should have sent Claudia with Amelia for submissiveness training.

Clean and having eaten a slice of bread and cheese under Claudia's supervision, Euodia felt her headache ease though her heartache did not lessen. She tore a second piece of bread into shreds and arranged the remaining cheese in an overlapping circle.

When and how had her relationship with Syntyche become so twisted? Not twisted, unpleasant. Broken? Strained? She settled on lost.

It felt like losing another mater—first her true mater, then Helena, her adopted mater, and now Syntyche, the sister-mater who'd cared for her, the one she'd turned to since she was ten.

And she'd lost her friends Paul and Clement. They would want nothing to do with her. Nor would the other believers. If Marcellus heard of this, would his faith suffer? He'd never want to associate with the other believers. Maybe she didn't want to either.

Had she also lost the Lord? She shrank from calling out to Him. He'd named her "Beloved," but she'd failed to obey Him. Again. Did He tire of her? If there was no answer this time, she could not bear it. If she called and He told her to find joy, she'd weep.

Ignoring Claudia's protests, Euodia stumbled back to bed and curled up, her toes cold. Even Linus had deserted her.

CHAPTER EIGHTEEN

Syntyche's feet showed signs of healing. The relationship with Euodia did not.

After a few days, when she could stand and hobble across the floor with Demi's support, Syntyche ensconced herself in the kitchen. The rhythm of chopping onions and garlic, carrots and potatoes into uniform pieces soothed her. She rubbed meat with extra pepper from the spice box Alex had given her, before covering it in a brine.

She kneaded dough, set it to prove, and then punched it down, imagining Clement's face carved on the surface. Pastries—sweet and savory—filled platters stacked atop each other. She baked until the shelves were filled, new supplies needed to be ordered, and even Ty could eat no more.

He'd left her in Demi's care with no questions for a week, longer than she'd expected. It was not a surprise when he entered her domain and gestured for Demi to leave them alone.

Ty glanced at her bare feet poking out from beneath her loose house stola. She didn't budge from the chair she'd pulled to a table. She transferred the risen dough from its bowl onto the table.

"They heal?"

"Slowly but not yet enough for sandals." Her toes curled at the thought of straps and hard soles.

"My steward told me your friend came to see how you are."

"I don't want to see anyone." The dough suffered a hard blow.

"Or know who came to ask about you? Or who came to tell me you'd left the city?"

"Correct."

"Synee, I'm going to hear what happened from someone else, or you can tell me."

"It doesn't concern you, Ty."

"You're my sister. It concerns me."

"Then go ask the sister you love. It concerns her too."

"I tried. She's not seeing anyone."

Startled, Syntyche glanced up. "She's not? Not even you?"

"No. I'm going to Clement unless you tell me."

Defeated, she sighed. "There was a letter from the Apostle Paul, the one who was arrested and flogged even though he was a Roman citizen. Did you know—"

"Synee. Distraction won't work."

"Fine." She slugged the dough. "He mentioned me and Euodia in the letter. A single sentence, that's all."

"Not flattering? A bit critical?"

Her hands stilled. "A bit." She waited for Ty to rage against her God and faith and the other believers. This time, she wouldn't defend them or argue with him.

"I'm sorry, Synee. Being criticized rightly or wrongly is hard to hear."

A salty tear dampened the harshly punished ball of dough.

"Ty." She choked over the lump in her throat and gripped the table's edge. "I don't know what to do."

"With our sister? Give her time." Ty tore off a chunk of bread. "She's always been one to retreat and then emerge stronger. You'll see. In a week, she won't remember this tiff." He bit into the steaming bread. "Mmm, good."

"It's been almost a week. I think we—I—may have lost her. I've never seen her so upset."

She did not confess that Euodia's anguished cries haunted her dreams throughout each night or that their sister turned to Malitta for comfort instead of her own sister. Nor could she admit she'd walked away from Euodia without a word or touch.

His chewing scrutiny unnerved her. Had her words disclosed what she meant to hide? He bit off another piece. Watched her. Swallowed. Licked his fingers. Watched her. Did he read her face? Know her thoughts?

"You like to talk about faith and your God and how He changes people." Ty pinched the bridge of his nose—his "I'm thinking" habit. "Will He help?"

If she hadn't been sitting, her knees would have buckled. Thoughts—like cinnamon laced through dough—swirled.

He would, of course. Or maybe. She'd made a mess of things with the little sister she'd promised to protect, abandoning her at her lowest moment. He'd offered forgiveness multiple times before for other wrongs, but how long could that continue?

Ty suggesting her faith might help was enough to joggle her mind. Did he say it to calm her or to spark a reaction? To annoy her or gauge her commitment? To challenge her faith or criticize her response?

All of a sudden, the why of Ty's asking if God would help her didn't matter. She knew the answer in the core of her being. Yes, He'd help. She needed only to ask.

Ty piled food on a bronze plate and after giving her a long, curious look, left the kitchen. Demi returned, gathered dirty dishes, and began to hum as she washed them.

Syntyche remained seated.

How did she ask for help? It had been so long, she struggled to remember. Should she begin by listing her faults? That might take forever, and He already knew each one.

Paul taught salvation came by faith in Christ's death and resurrection. She did not doubt her salvation. Did forgiving those who wronged her also come by faith?

She pushed herself to think, to remember, to understand.

Jesus said that one must forgive to be forgiven. But how? How to release the pain others inflicted, the relentless yearning for an apology that never arrived?

Her hand clutching the table cramped. She'd gripped the edge so tightly each finger had to be pried loose with her other hand. It hurt. Cautiously, she flexed her fingers. The pain lessened until it was only a memory.

"Lord, hear my cry. The pain is too much. Help me forgive, wrest me away from the grudges, the resentments, the wrongs

I hold on to. Whatever it takes for You to forgive me, for Euodia to forgive me, I will bear."

One hurt, one grievance, one rejection at a time, Syntyche boldly brought each to the Lord and imagined Him taking it from her. With every touch of His hand, pain diminished. And though she remembered each wrong, she sensed they'd no longer control her.

Euodia burrowed deeper into the comfort of her pillows to escape the ruckus. The squabbling outside her room broke through her dreams. Covering her ears muffled the sound until what sounded like a slap and ensuing shriek roused her enough to drag herself from bed, plod across the room, and open the door.

"What is happening?" Her sleep-clogged murmur emerged as a croak.

There was no evidence of a slap or tears or even anger among the three servants. Claudia's "Did we disturb you, mistress? I'm so sorry" sounded less than concerned and not at all contrite. They'd contrived a plot to wake her?

She narrowed her eyes at them in an attempt to sound stern. "Have you nothing to do other than bicker and quarrel outside my door while I'm sleeping?"

Claudia shooed the other two servants away. "Now that you're awake, come and show us what you want done with the clutter Amelia's slaves left."

"I don't care. Send it to her. All of it." Euodia tried to close the door.

Claudia's foot remained over the threshold. "They are your things, not hers, except for a few items I don't recognize. We just uncovered them in the storage area. At least come look at them so we know what you want done and are of the same mind."

Euodia flinched under the sting of those words.

"Oh, I almost forgot. Master Marcellus sent word he hopes to return late tonight or tomorrow morning."

Marcellus. Euodia suppressed a groan. Pretending all was well in front of her husband's eagle eyes would take a lot of effort. She looked at her rumpled bed with longing. If she was sleeping when he returned—

"Mistress, please?" Claudia's voice wavered. "Please come back to us. We need you."

The plea broke through the barrier of her grief. Though unacceptable between mistress and maid, she held out her arms to Claudia. She'd wallowed long enough and let her servants carry the burden. Her disgrace might soon be known throughout her household, but she needn't add selfishness to her shame.

Releasing Claudia, she retreated to her room, washed her face, and donned a loose house stola. Linus pranced in for a scratch then scampered out the door. At least someone still loved her, even if it was a dog.

Claudia followed her, tidying the room and straightening the bed as Euodia readied herself. "Felix and his wife dragged the crates into the room Mistress Amelia used. It's swept, and we can sort things into piles on the floor."

Euodia nodded approval.

"I think they took armloads of your things and dumped them into the crates. I can't make any sense of it." Claudia replaced the cup by Euodia's bed with a fresh one. "And they were in such a hurry, they left some of their things too."

"Gather everyone except Tira and Cook. Have Tira stay by the front door in case Marcellus sends another message. If he does, have her bring it to me immediately."

She walked determinedly to Amelia's room, eager to see this mess that needed sorting. Organizing chaos, placing like with like, and deciding what to do with each object helped her think things through, make decisions, and bring order to her life. After the world-tumbling humiliation of Paul's censure, making sense of anything was a welcome task.

The room held more crates than she'd expected. If they were all hers and she hadn't missed these things in the time Amelia had been here, maybe she didn't need all of them.

The sun teetered on the horizon before they'd emptied and sorted the crates and bags. Dented silver was boxed for repair. A sack of ribbons and pins she'd sort through later had spilled at her feet. Clay cups and basins were collected on trays to be sent to the kitchen for Cook to keep or discard. A box containing Amelia's lists was ordered to be burned.

Unfamiliar scarves and pallas were folded and stacked to distribute among the poor of Philippi. Linus claimed a stray sandal to chew. A vase that had been her mater's was returned to its place of honor. Irreparable bits and pieces swept into a heap waited to be thrown away.

Euodia stood from her place in the middle of the piles and brushed her hands against her wrinkled stola. Tomorrow, each pile would be sent to its new home and out of her house. She started to declare the day's work complete when Tira's frantic pleas reached her ears.

"No. Lady, you have to leave. You can't just walk in here. Stop. Please, stop. No one is allowed entrance."

Syntyche! Euodia's heart surged. Had her sister come to make amends? Oh, how she wanted to see her, to run into welcoming arms and share a sister hug in spite of the ocean of hurt between them.

Tira walked backward, dancing in front of a person Euodia did not wish to see.

Helena.

She thinned her lips. "Tira, I will deal with this. Go with the others to eat and rest. It is not your fault, child. Be at peace."

Abashed, Helena offered a tremulous smile. "The child tried very hard to keep me from entering your home, but I was determined to see you, Euodia."

"So it seems."

With a flutter of her fingers, Euodia dismissed her servants.

When all had left the room, even Claudia, who hesitated and raised a questioning eyebrow before taking Tira by the hand, Euodia crossed her arms and turned toward Helena. Waited.

Helena cleared her throat. "I came to say…to tell you…to let you know…" She twisted the sides of her stola. "I…you are dear to me, and I know I hurt you." She looked down and then raised her head. "Please forgive me. Let us be at peace with one another."

Euodia remained motionless, guarded. Helena's unexpected appearance and contrite words were too soon. She yet reeled from the public correction and betrayal by both Paul and Clement.

Into her silence, Helena continued to speak. "Later in Paul's letter—it was after he said your name—I'm not sure you heard that he thanked us for the gift we sent. Euodia, a large part of that gift were the coins you sent in the embroidered purse. I thought you'd like to know it went to Paul to purchase food and ease his imprisonment."

Helena reached out a hand. Euodia ignored it.

"You are not ready to speak with me. I realize that now, but Brother Syzygus sends word that he hurts for you, and when you are ready to heal, he will come to you as quickly as you will allow. Clement, also, will come if you'd rather speak to him.

"I'm sorry to have barged in, but I'd hoped... I suppose I should have waited for the Lord's direction. I'll see myself to the door. Please do not scold the child. She did her best."

Ready to heal.

She clenched her fists, the words unsettling her. Who would not want to heal after being struck down and left bruised and bleeding? Thoughts of those she'd tended crowded in: Cerberus, mal aria victims, Noah with his despondency, Valeria, infants struggling for breath, the woman with a broken hip, the young widow. All of them either chose to fight for healing or surrendered to dependency or death.

Ready to heal? How dare anyone say that to her? She huffed indignantly. Of course she was ready to heal. Who would not be eager to be whole and pain free?

An image came—of a child's broken arm and the awareness in a parent's eye when she explained that straightening it would hurt horribly, but leaving it twisted would hurt forever.

Ready to heal? Maybe not. The thought of her wound being probed turned her stomach. She'd wait until the ache of this initial brokenness dulled before she submitted to the pain of healing. After all, no one knew how badly she hurt. Outwardly, she appeared well, if the weight loss and skin pallor went unnoticed.

She unclenched her fists in defeat. She of all people knew the longer a brokenness was ignored, the more painful to set it right. She was as injured and hurting as her patients and in desperate need of a healer. Only One knew the depth of her pain and shame. Only one held the power of healing.

"Lord?"

Beloved.

So quickly He answered. She sank to the floor amid the piles of discards and rubbish. Wept.

Others might see her as disgraced.

She might feel unworthy.

But her Lord named her Beloved.

"Heal me."

Joy.

She laughed in spite of tears drenching her face. *Joy* must be His favorite word.

"Yes, Lord."

She leaned into the long-missing peace.

CHAPTER NINETEEN

September

Yesterday had been Rosh Hashanah. Syntyche wondered who might have prepared the feast. There were other good cooks and good bakers, but no one did both as well as she did. It was not pride speaking the words. It was an acknowledged fact. If she did run a *thermopolium* as Ty had accused, it would be a thriving business.

Had her cooking skills been missed, or was there such relief at her absence no one cared if the food was not perfect?

In ten days, there would be another feast, a feast of new beginnings, and since she wanted to prepare it as a thanksgiving for God's forgiveness and as an apology to the other believers, she needed to speak with Clement and receive his permission. It was impossible to dread anything more than facing him.

Peace in their community was paramount to Clement, and she'd disrupted it. He would be stern, exhorting her to repent and do penance, and relentless as he listed the consequences of her actions and those who had suffered from her dispute with Euodia. No excuse would explain answering to herself rather than her Lord. Whatever he said or demanded, she'd remain contrite and humble.

She packed a basket of fresh breads and pastries as a peace offering. It would not make everything right, but it never hurt to offer food to an angry man. If it seemed he'd refuse her gesture of peace, she'd say they were for Helena. At least someone could enjoy the treats.

She dressed with care, and for the first time since that awful day, she strapped on sandals. Ty's steward had taken the carriage to have a wheel repaired, but if she walked gingerly, she could make it to Clement's house and back.

The sun had not yet warmed the day, or else the chill inside prevented her from feeling any warmth. She shivered, wishing she could have used Ty's carriage. She dodged a pair of pigeons pecking at the ground in search of crumbs. As she walked, she composed her apology.

First, she'd offer the baked goods. Then she'd hold her head high and look him in the eye and say, "Brother Clement, I'm here to humbly offer my wholehearted and heartfelt, deepest apology to you and to the church for..." No. Too many words. She'd say "I'm sorry. How do I make restitution?" Too abrupt. Maybe a different question. "Brother Clement, what do you think Paul meant by 'one mind'?" Too defensive.

Lost in planning her approach, she stood before Clement's house before she knew it. Still uncertain of what to say, she tapped the door softly. Maybe no one was home.

Instead of a servant, Clement opened the door when she knocked. She wasn't sure who was more surprised. Their gazes locked. Did he see her remorse? Did he see *her*?

She dropped her gaze. "Brother Clement, may I talk with you?"

Without a word, he opened the door wider, moving back as she stepped into the warmth of the house. She handed the basket to a nearby servant, slipped off her sandals, and followed him to his office.

"Please sit down. I'm glad to see you, Syntyche, glad you are here."

The tenderness undid her composure. Unexpectedly, tears moistened her eyes then spilled, drenching her cheeks. An ugly, face-scrunched, wrenching sob followed. She covered her mouth.

"I'm so sorry for the trouble I've caused you, for the embarrassment to the church and for living to please myself instead of our Lord."

A cloth was pressed into her hand. She dabbed at her eyes, trying to stanch the tears.

"I have asked and received the Lord's forgiveness. Can you forgive me? Will my sister ever forgive me? Will the other believers and Paul?"

His silence frightened her.

She raised her head. He'd come from behind his desk and knelt in front of her, his eyes tender bright with unshed tears.

"Syntyche, the Lord forgives me each day for my mistakes. How could I not forgive you, dear sister?"

She sobbed harder. "I have been so f-f-full of pride, but I'm no b-better than anyone else." She wiped her eyes and nose with the cloth. "I'm so ashamed, Clement. How can I face the others?"

"That's still pride, Syntyche. With so many turning to me for guidance and teaching, I struggle with that too. You and I, we must show the others we have learned to live as ones forgiven, not as perfect people."

He cradled her hand between his two strong ones. "Today your visit and words have brought a healing to me. If you have the strength to confess your wrongs in this, so must I."

Almost afraid to move, Syntyche tilted her head, unsure she'd heard correctly. His wrongs?

"It would have been kinder had I shared with you and Euodia in private."

"But maybe not as effective." Her attempt at a brave smile failed. "The other churches who receive the letter will also read it aloud and learn from those words." Forlorn, she dropped her head. "My sin is forgiven but will always be remembered by believers."

"Yes, but you don't see them and work alongside them. They do not know your face. The ones who know you will see the change. What they will remember is your teachable spirit and willingness to obey Paul's admonition."

He reached for her other hand and held both securely within his own. "Paul must have known you and Euodia are strong enough to bear the correction, that you'd respond in the way of a true leader, one that continues to teach others."

"Clement, I tire of being the strong one, of feeling that I am always watched, that I must be sensible and brave, that my honesty is seen as too harsh. I tire of struggling alone in my faith."

"Maybe someday you will not need to walk it alone."

He did not release her hands. She did not pull away.

"Clement, there is more I must confess. I do not understand how to be of one mind with Euodia. We are so different. How can we be in agreement?"

He opened his hands, cupped them so hers rested inside. "Syntyche, I know nothing of measuring and roasting and baking breads. Can you design a building and order what's needed for its completion like I do?"

"No."

"Different callings. Different skills. You trust me to use my gifts as I trust you to use yours."

"That is being of one mind?"

He smiled and squeezed her hands. "It is when we work for the same cause in love and respect."

Leaving the kitchen after a meeting with Cook about preparing more vegetables and fish, Euodia halted midstep. Brother Syzygus sat in her atrium, his wispy hair wind-mussed, his hem and sandals muddy.

"No one answered the door, so I let myself inside. The Lord told me to speak with you today, so I must."

He looked so pleased with himself that she smiled.

"Welcome, Brother. May I offer you refreshment?"

"No, child. I have the Lord's message for you, and then I'll be on my way. Will you sit with me?"

Euodia crossed to where he patted the bench and sat beside him on the turquois silk.

He shook a swollen, crooked finger in her face. "You missed the feast of Rosh Hashanah. It was wonderful but not as splendid as it could have been. Two of my favorite people were not there."

He paused and looked at her from the corner of his eye. "Ask me who."

"Who?"

"You and your sister."

She looked away.

"I am not the only one who missed you. Ask me who else missed you."

He was enjoying his game, so she complied. "Who else?"

"Clement was downcast."

"Oh."

"I think he especially missed your sister. I missed you." His eyes twinkled. "Clement told me the wonderful news about your husband. When will he join us in worship?"

Her shoulders drooped. "Brother Syzygus, from my example, he believes he can follow Christ and not tell anyone."

"Then you must give him a new example, dear. It's a very simple solution." He took her hand. "Euodia, I know you hurt. You are downcast and believe yourself disgraced. It is not so."

Not so? Her foot began to twitch, swishing her hem against the floor. She most certainly was disgraced and humiliated and hurt and a failure.

"Child, it was a simple correction—not a condemnation—a plea from Paul's heart because you are so precious to him, so valuable to this church, and so beloved of our Lord Jesus. You, in all your strength and gifts, are profoundly needed."

He tapped his lips and stroked the length of his beard. "There was something else I came to tell you...something. Something about food. Oh, yes. You and your sister are to prepare the feast at the end of the ten Days of Awe. Now, I go to tell your sister she must help you prepare the feast or you must help her. I'm not sure which, but you must begin tomorrow. You will go, yes?"

"Yes."

"Peace be with you."

Syzygus ambled from the atrium and out the door, leaving another trail of muddy footprints and Euodia dazed. Why had she agreed without thinking?

She and Syntyche? Working together? So soon? Her rediscovered peace crumbled around the corners like parchment catching fire.

"Lord? And please don't say joy."

Peace.

Euodia closed her eyes, spread wide her arms, and breathed in the word's delicate fragrance. Peace with her Lord. And someday—maybe—peace with her sister.

She'd let nothing and no one ever again steal her peace.

"Euodia? What are you doing?" Marcellus's face was comical in its confusion.

Startled, she giggled. If she told Marcellus she was breathing in peace, he'd summon a physician.

"Breathing."

He tilted his head the way Linus did when unsure of what she wanted. Evidently, he expected her to say more. She didn't.

"Oh." He shook his head. "During this last trip, I met a friend of yours, or rather the husband of your friend." He sat beside her. "Do you know a Valeria?"

Euodia squirmed. "Yes, and I need to tell you—"

Marcellus interrupted her with an upheld hand. "Our house looks like our house. When did this happen? It was dark, and I didn't notice when I returned home this morning." He perused the walls and furnishings. "My parents' belongings are gone." He angled toward her. "Euodia, where are my parents?"

"Your mater returned to the villa after I visited with Valeria. It was a sudden departure. She was distressed when she left."

He swiveled to face her.

When she finished the story, he lowered his head and covered his face.

"I'm so sorry, Marcellus. I will do whatever I can to make amends with them. I knew beyond doubt Valeria did not have leprosy, but your mater refused to believe me."

His shoulders began to shake. A choking sound emerged from behind his hands and then he threw back his head and whooped. "Leprosy! It took the threat of leprosy to move her out of here. I doubt she'll ever return." He jumped to his feet, lifted her in his arms, and spun her in a circle.

"You're not angry?" Dizzy, she held on tightly.

"I love my parents, but when they moved in and took over, it angered me. Why do you think I've been on so many trips while they were here?" He sobered. "And wrongly left you to handle them. I'm sorry, Euodia. Forgive me?"

When he looked at her like that, there was nothing she'd not forgive.

Euodia wrapped a tendril of Marcellus's hair around her finger as he slept. When he opened one eye and smiled, she believed him more beautiful than any sculpture of a god she'd ever seen.

"I'm relieved you're not angry about your mater's departure."

"Not at all. It's good to come home to my house and my wife."

"You started to tell me of meeting Valeria's husband."

He rolled over on his back and cushioned his head on his folded arms. "He recognized me from Juno's feast and remembered you and his wife were close friends."

"Not exactly friends."

"He'd just returned from Rome and the turmoil there and warned it's becoming more dangerous by the day. Nero had his mater killed because she opposed his new lover."

"He killed his mater? Marcellus, how terrible."

"Then exiled his wife, Octavia."

Euodia propped herself up on one elbow. "Was she unfaithful? Treasonous?"

"He divorced her because she gave him no child, but I understand it was never an easy marriage, and that was just an excuse to rid himself of her so he could be with his lover."

"The poor woman."

"He divorced his wife, accused her of adultery, had her murdered, and then married his lover."

"He murdered her? Why, if they were divorced?"

Marcellus gathered Euodia in his arms. "It makes no sense, but this man—our emperor—does as he pleases with no control."

He tightened his arms around her. "Murder changes a person. Nero might have tried to end taxes, and yes, he is a patron of the arts, but he has unleashed evil within himself. There will be more murders, more brutality. He's a vicious man who retaliates against all who do not ingratiate themselves to him."

Euodia shuddered. "At least we are safe here in Philippi. I never want to be anywhere near him."

"Nor do I, and yet with the commission, I must travel to Rome and—"

"No. Please don't go. Decline the commission and stay here with me."

"Euodia, you know I'm not going to turn down that opportunity, but I'll tread carefully. To slip into Nero's shadowed side is to invite destruction. He is loving and tolerant until he is not, and then he is vindictive and cruel."

Euodia covered her ears. "Enough ugliness for a beautiful morning. I have something to share but first a request to ask of you."

"It will delight me to say yes to whatever you ask." He tapped the tip of her nose. "Ask."

"Next week, a feast will be held for all believers. Will you go with me? I promise the food will be splendid." She batted her eyes. "Syntyche and I are preparing it."

He raised a beautifully arched eyebrow. "Dearest, did you not understand the meaning of Valeria's husband's warning? Nero is going mad. This is not the time to publicly align ourselves with Christ followers. They refuse to worship Nero. Sooner or later, he will turn on them, and it will be uglier than anything the world has ever seen."

Sitting up, she tried to catch and hold his attention. "Marcellus, part of faith is being with other believers to encourage them as they grow spiritually and share in their joys. You have come to faith, have you not?"

"Yes, my dear. Absolutely. I have come to faith in our Lord Jesus. He is my Savior, and I worship no other. But I cannot commit to being a known part of His followers. Besides, you know most are ruffians and rabble."

Marcellus kissed the top of her head and left their bed. "I will be working until late this evening. Don't wait up for me."

She watched him prepare for the day. Beneath the covers, she cradled her belly, suddenly hesitant to tell him of the child she suspected grew within. How did one commit and not commit? Would he stay by her side and by their child when she refused to withdraw from believers' fellowship?

Linus jumped on the bed and nuzzled her ear. If only everyone was as faithful and unreservedly committed as her little dog. Did dogs regret their choices like people did? What was she thinking to have promised Syzygus she'd work with her sister?

She flopped backward on the bed, the churning in her stomach different from that which had plagued her for the last three months. According to Brother Syzygus, today she must not only face Syntyche but work alongside her.

What did one say to a sister absolutely adored yet wholeheartedly resented, when the Lord has directed *joy*?

"Good morning, I'd rather be anywhere but here. Can we please make up?"

Or, "Do you love and dislike me as much as I do you?"

Maybe, "Can we go back to pretending?"

Each possibility was truth, and not a single one was what she wanted to say. "Lord?"

Joy.

Of course He'd say that.

Joy? She closed her eyes and searched deep inside. It would be joy to say, "Hear who I am. Show me you value me. Let me see who you are behind your facade of perfection. Is it possible to be friends as well as sisters?"

Maybe someday she'd have the courage to say those words. Today, all her courage would be tapped to look her sister in the eye.

CHAPTER TWENTY

Syntyche smoothed the parchment of her shopping list. She'd decided the menu, compiled the needed ingredients, and created a plan to complete it in time. There were only seven more days until the feast of new beginnings.

How had Euodia responded to Brother Syzygus when informed she'd be helping her with the preparations? Had she refused, or was she willing? Dreading it or eager to reconcile? Did she intend to help or ignore the message to work with her?

She rubbed her eyes. So much to purchase and prepare. She could manage it alone. She didn't want to.

She wanted to stand beside her sister while cooking and share stories of their childhood, of Tymon finding a secret passage beneath the house and Euodia hiding under the sofa to listen to the adults, of sneaking sweets while Mater's back was turned and how each month, she woke her little sister to slip out into the night to see the full moon. She longed to revisit the days of serving alongside Paul when the joy of knowing the Messiah warmed their souls and poured out of every word and action.

Working together wasn't going to happen unless one of them reached out to the other. If Euodia was too stubborn to come to her, she'd go to Euodia.

"Demi."

The curly-headed girl popped around the corner.

"I'm going out. Can you pull the potatoes out of the oven in an hour?"

"And peel them?"

"No. Leave them alone. I don't want you to burn your fingers and have scars all over your hands like mine. Use a towel to handle them."

She tied on her shoes with only a hint of a grimace, flung on a palla, and left before she changed her mind. The closer she drew to Euodia's home, the slower she walked. Maybe it would have been wiser asking a go-between like Clement or Tymon to speak with her sister or waiting for Euodia to reach out or just planning to do all the work herself.

She paused outside Euodia's home and surveyed the steps to the entrance—each, a mountain to scale, looming taller than the one before. Not much daunted her, but confronting another irate merchant in the forum appealed more than facing the little sister she'd hurt.

"Lord, what do I say to her? That You forgave me so she must? That I'll never leave her again? How do I make this right? What does she want from me?"

Listen.

"That I can do. I'll listen without a word of interruption for as long as she wants to talk."

The door opened. Euodia, followed by a servant, stepped out and hesitated atop the stairs, looking down at her.

Motionless, they gazed at each other, neither smiling, neither reaching out.

Syntyche ached as forever passed. Lost days. Months of misunderstanding. Years of silent comparison. Heartsick, she saw the hollows of Euodia's face, the lines etched where before there had been none, the guarded look in her sister's eyes. Her sparkle had dimmed, and she, Syntyche, was responsible.

"Euodia, I've come to ask if you will please help me prepare the second feast."

"Brother Syzygus said I must."

Syntyche flinched at the emotionless response. It was a yes, but an ugly, resigned yes. Keeping her voice steady, she asked, "Where is best for us to work, your house, mine, or Sister Helena's?"

"No! Not hers."

Syntyche wondered at the force behind the no.

"Cook does not like to share her kitchen. Yours is fine. I was going there, anyway."

To say, "you are no longer my sister"? Hope bubbled up when those words were not forthcoming. Maybe Euodia came to talk or make peace.

"Claudia, you may stay. I'll walk with…her."

Syntyche winced at the refusal to say her name or claim relationship. Hope drifted away—a fallen leaf bereft of its anchor.

Euodia descended the steps and walked silently next to Syntyche.

"I made a list and went to the market. I think I have all the spices and herbs. You've always had a better hand seasoning vegetables than I. Would you prepare those dishes?"

Euodia shrugged. "As you wish."

Entering the kitchen before her, Euodia paused in the doorway as if the aromas of delicate pastries and roasted meat, baked potatoes and chopped garlic, mint tea and crisping ginger brought a swell of memories.

Did it comfort? Did it remind her of the hours here with Mater and then just the two of them—a time not so long ago that might be forever lost?

Syntyche motioned toward a chair. "We have only seven days including today. We haven't much time, since it is just the two of us and Demi. Feeding so many people is a lot of work."

They sat at the table opposite each other. Euodia kept her eyes focused on the list, nodding or murmuring an occasional one-word response.

Syntyche clicked her short nails against the table. *Lord, how do I listen if she won't talk and tell me what she needs from me or what she's thinking?*

Listen.

She'd not dare roll her eyes at God, despite the temptation.

Listen to what? Syntyche fidgeted in frustration. Thinking back, she remembered Euodia saying she knew how people felt or what they thought by watching hands and shoulders, lips and eyes.

She looked hard at her sister. Euodia's hands, in front of her on the table, gripped each other like a shield. Her shoulders—high. Her eyes—wary. Did she expect to be attacked? Her lips were pressed thin and flat as if an unguarded word might escape.

Eyes downcast, lips tight, Euodia said not a word, but Syntyche heard her and almost doubled over in remorse. Her gentle, sparkly little sister sat stoically like a reprimanded child awaiting further punishment. Had Euodia decided relationship with her sister was too great a risk? If Euodia refused to talk, how could they ever be of one mind?

Her voice tight, Syntyche reached across the table, hands outstretched. "Sister, I wronged you."

Euodia looked up, eyes guarded, and drew back.

"I hope someday you'll forgive me, that we will share peace."

Euodia remained silent. Did she give an infinitesimal nod, or did Syntyche see what she wanted to see?

Euodia refused Syntyche's offer of the carriage in spite of the sky softening to the blue of early twilight. A cool gust of wind billowed her skirts with a promise of more to come. There would not be too many more days like this. In another month, the weather would turn brisk. Soon it would be too cold to walk for the joy of being outside and free from watching eyes.

Nor did she want an immediate return to running her home, with its demands and expectations. She longed for solitude, a respite to unfold and smooth the creases of long ago hurts, the wrinkle of rash words, the emotional upheaval of being with her sister.

Odd to have sat across from Syntyche instead of beside her. Unheard of to be asked instead of told. Comforting to smell the crisping ginger. Healing to be asked for forgiveness. It was almost as if, finally, Syntyche saw her, heard her wordless cries.

Is that where healing began?

The apology, the reaching out, told her Syntyche wanted healing between them—as did she—yet in that moment, fear had wrapped itself around her, stealing her words and warning against meeting Syntyche halfway. Every hurtful word her sister ever said had roared through her mind, distorting what was spoken today.

After the morning together, they were no closer to peace, and she did not know if they ever would be. The Lord's joy seemed far away.

Somewhere in the distance, workers called to each other. A vivid memory from years ago swept over her. In the forum with its milling crowds and multiple shops of colors and aromas and everyone going in a different direction, losing sight of someone happened often, especially if one was small and easily distracted by shining trinkets. After numerous scoldings from Syntyche and her own tearful howls whenever they became separated, Syntyche had developed a signal—a bird's warbling call—for them to locate each other and reunite.

How oddly people had reacted when she raised her little voice and warbled the call. How comforting to hear her call echoed and know the safety of her sister was an arm's length away or close behind her.

If only she could warble out her heart's call, assured Syntyche would respond, and they'd find each other through the chaos separating them, the differences dividing them. Then all would be well.

They'd been through so much together—the scant years, their parents' death, meeting Paul, accepting Christ, working to spread the Gospel, Syntyche losing husband, child, and home, Marcellus's parents' dislike of her, and now the public correction from Paul.

She'd prefer to blame Syntyche for the distance between them. After all, she was older and had worked alongside Paul for longer stretches. Fine. A few longer days, but still…longer.

She grimaced. If she was honest, she too was at fault. That thought fled as she approached her home. Near the entrance stood a carriage with a single horse. Foreboding as cold as December's wind swept over her. Slowly, she climbed the steps and opened the door to what ought to have been a haven. Aghast, she stared at the one before her. Not today. Not her.

Helena.

The small woman's white head was bowed over her clasped hands as if in prayer, her growing frailty pronounced in the near translucent skin. And yet an intangible strength glowed from within—a power drawing Euodia closer, preventing her from an attempt to flee before her guest realized she was here.

Unsettled, Euodia spoke into the silence. "Sister Helena."

"Daughter."

Such grief and longing packed into one word. Euodia wavered between running to fall on her knees and rest her head in Helena's lap or folding her arms and standing firm. She did neither. She stammered a welcome. Hurt was not easy to forgive nor indifference easy to maintain.

Helena's eyes twinkled.

"Probably not truly welcome, but it was a gracious attempt. I will speak with you and then leave. If you never wish to see me again, I understand, because what I am going to say is difficult to speak and will be difficult to hear."

Who was this Helena? Gone were the scolding words, and there was a confidence she'd never seen in the older woman.

"Sit with me, dear." Helena smoothed the silk cushion beside her. "For just a moment."

Euodia forced herself to move closer but kept enough distance between them that she could not be touched. She ignored the sadness that reached across Helena's face.

"Euodia, you have become a woman of beauty and grace."

That was not hard to hear. Suspicious, she slanted her eyes at Helena. What else was coming?

"A woman of more talents than most, who gives generously and without judgment."

But?

Criticism always followed a compliment. She braced for a listing of her faults.

"You have a single fault." Helena chuckled. "I'm wishing the same could be said for me—to only have a single fault."

Euodia waited, stone-faced.

"Allow me to tell you a story. We are very alike, so perhaps you can discern your fault."

Really? Euodia folded her lips inward to prevent disrespect and annoyance from spewing out. A guessing game of her fault?

Helena tsked. "I'm annoying you, but grant me a quick listen and then I'll be gone. You've stood beside me singing praise to our Lord, so you know my singing—with mercy—can be called a joyful noise. I'm not skilled with numbers nor needlework. Neither can I draw nor write a legible sentence. But I can read."

She scooted forward as if imparting a secret. "Few know that I am able to memorize pages by the dozen. Once I see a sheet of words, they are etched in my mind, as permanent as if chiseled on a stone."

Surprised out of her resentment, Euodia turned toward Helena. "That's incredible. I'd give anything to remember each word in Paul's letters."

Lines crinkled across the thin forehead. "Euodia, do you understand? If everyone were like me, we'd have no music to sing nor beauty on our walls. And if everyone created the art your Marcellus does, we'd run out of walls and gardens to display it."

"I suppose, but being able to remember so much is a wonderful gift."

Helena cocked her head like a little bird and peered at Euodia. "Maybe to you, but my mater excelled at everything I did not and saw no use for my odd skill except in memorizing recipes. For years, she saw me as useless. I believed myself worthless."

"No, Helena, even if you did not have that gift of memory, you are caring and kind to everyone you meet."

"Not always kind, as you well know." She reddened. "But that's for another time."

Euodia stiffened and glanced away. She too was reluctant to revisit the hurt of that day.

Helena continued. "I was blind to my value and, dear, you do not see your value. Your fault is blindness."

"Nonsense. I'm not blind at all." Euodia lifted her chin. "I know my healing skills are needed and valued. You are mistaken. We are nothing alike."

"You are blind when you compare yourself to Syntyche, who is also a woman of many talents but different ones. Yours are not less than hers. Hers are not less than yours. They are different. Both are necessary. The world does not need two Syntyches nor two Euodias." Her lips curved ruefully. "And certainly not two of me, although two Clements would be nice."

When Euodia did not respond, Helena took a deep breath and forged ahead. "Comparing yourself to her—or anyone—creates resentment or pride and that leads to strife and discouragement and blindness."

Helena leaned back and looked upward as if thinking. "I admit some comparison is good. I compare my balms and unguents to yours and seek to improve them. I've always admired the way you drape your stola and sometimes try to copy that, but that's different. It encourages me to do better. It does not cause me to feel less than you."

"But Syntyche—"

"Is how God made her." Her eyes sharpened. "Do you criticize the Almighty for how He created you?"

"No." She twitched her foot. "Maybe. I wish…I don't know what I wish."

Helena slid closer to Euodia but refrained from touching her.

"Dear child, dear sister in Christ, I pray that our Lord will set you free from the shackles you've forged for yourself, the scales you've pasted over your eyes. Whether they prevent you from accepting your worth or accepting your sister's worth—and only our Lord knows your heart—they are rooted in pride, the desire to be of more value than another or believe another is of more worth than you."

"I am not prideful." She spat the words, glowering at her guest.

Helena raised a pale eyebrow. "You have never wished your sister to be more like you?"

"Nor do I compare myself to her."

"Ahh. You have never tried to be more like her? Paul's plea for—"

Euodia stood abruptly, her face burning with fury. "I'm tired, Helena. It's been a long day. Allow me to see you out."

Helena rose, her face serene. "I have spoken all the words the Lord gave me except these. There are seven days left of the Days of Awe. Seven days before we celebrate a new beginning. What will you do with your remaining days?" She dipped her head. "I leave you in peace, Euodia."

Euodia scowled as the door closed behind Helena.

"No, you do not leave me in peace. You leave me angry and confused and in more turmoil than before."

Euodia brushed past Claudia and stormed to the solitude of the garden. She paced the length of the garden, snapping the heads off any rose looking askance at her, mumbling to herself.

"Peace? Telling me I'm prideful brings peace? No comfort, no assurance of her friendship, no sympathy from a loving friend?"

Raising her voice as if Helena could hear her, she declared, "I have no need of friends like you."

No one responded. "Am I closer to finding peace with my sister? No. I'm just carrying more criticism, more thorns. And to say her words were from the Lord! I think not."

She pivoted, retracing the way she'd come.

"The Lord speaks 'Peace.' Helena arrives to censure me. Both cannot be from the Lord. Impossible. They don't go together."

She fingered a rough cuticle, held it against her tongue to soften it, and then chewed it. She almost heard Syntyche's scolding to keep her fingers out of her mouth.

"Blind to my fault. Wrong. I know my every fault. I'm too timid. I can't sing. I'm easily distracted. I can continue listing them all day and night, and if I forget something, Syntyche can fill in the blank because she is perfect."

Syntyche. Euodia caught her breath. Helena was right.

She did compare herself to Syntyche. She always had. It was natural, wasn't it? A little sister trying and failing to do the grown-up things her older sister did. A quiet child in awe of her older sister's vivacious confidence and eloquence. A different person afraid she wouldn't be worth keeping if her skills, her gifts were not valued, not as worthy as her sister's.

Euodia flopped on a bench and stared unseeing in the fading light of the garden.

"Seven days to make peace with a lifetime of being not quite enough. Seven days until we return to church and a new beginning where our every word and gesture will be scrutinized to see if we accepted Paul's admonishment and discovered how to be of one mind."

Seven days to swallow her pride—yes, pride—and work with Syntyche, who oversaw and managed everything she did. If only Syntyche spoke softer, allowed her to think for herself, looked beyond the obvious to the unsaid, treated her with respect and kindness. Seven days with Syntyche. "Fine, Lord. Tell me how."

Joy.

"Good heavens, not that again."

She folded pleats in the loose drapes of her stola, crossed both arms and legs. Her fingers drummed, her foot swished against the garden pavers.

"Seven days to be at peace—"

A burst of insight pierced her thoughts with a lightning bolt of clarity. She caught her breath. Whispered, "—with myself."

Imperfect though she was.

Proud. Jealous.

Yet in His truth, beloved, redeemed.

She singled out a fear, and trembling, held it up to His truth, the lie recognized and named. Illuminated by a holy light, distortion vanished, the fear dissipated. For a long time, she sat in the darkened garden, digging for the root of each fear, surrendering it to Him.

Claudia brought a lamp, a shawl for warmth, a cup of water, and set each on the marble bench beside her before returning to the house. Neither woman spoke.

Her giftings, her worth glowed when not compared against her insecurities or another's strengths. In Him, she was complete, her value unshakeable. She did not need to be Syntyche, only Euodia.

She marveled at the new depth of understanding and her spirit's joy. She laughed. Joy!

"Lord, this is what You meant—to find joy in You and who You created me to be."

Kneeling on the cool stones by the bench, she gave thanks for the gift of joy and the promise of peace. At peace with her Lord. At peace with herself. Surely peace with Syntyche would follow. If they were at peace, would they be of one mind?

CHAPTER TWENTY-ONE

Syntyche woke early after a restless night. She'd dreamed of her infant daughter and awakened wondering who the tiny beloved would have become, what would have made her giggle, if she'd have enjoyed learning to bake and cook.

Resolutely, she tucked away the unanswerable questions, the timeless grief, and forced herself to sit up, to stretch the kinks from her back. With only a few days left before the feast, the preparations pressed in on her, the most important task finding a way to prevent another loss and mend the rift with Euodia.

Granted, it was more than a rift. It was a lifetime of—secretly—considering herself better than her sister. Not always, but often.

She admired Euodia's selflessness and her soft-spoken demeanor—envied her understanding of herbs in the healing arts. Euodia's ability to hear the unspoken and see beyond a person's mask amazed her.

Tilting the scale was the annoyance of Euodia's myriad fears, her desire to keep the peace and please all people—an impossibility. The patience with which she endured her in-laws, and that dreadful Valeria, was beyond Syntyche's understanding.

She swung her legs over the edge of the bed, rested her feet on the ground to test their healing. Satisfied, she washed her face and dressed in an under-tunic and her oldest house stola.

With its half sleeve, it was suitable for a day in the kitchen. After braiding her hair, she glanced in the mirror to confirm all strands were securely out of her face. Nothing worse than finding a long hair in an otherwise perfect meal.

Last night before she left for home, Demi had set out a chunk of bread and a saucer of olive oil, covering both with a clean towel. Syntyche didn't know Demi's story—Euodia would have known—but she was grateful for the bubbly, curly-haired girl's service.

She glanced outside at the sun. Would Euodia return today to help? With so much to do, she couldn't wait for her sister.

After hefting a bag of ground wheat to her worktable, she measured handfuls of flour, mixed in eggs and salt and yeast but no butter or milk. Aaron had mentioned the challah bread was braided, so she divided the dough into six portions and began to work each strand until all were twisted together. A sprinkle of flour on top, and it was set aside to rise. Immediately, she began another loaf and then another. Each day she'd bake three or four more loaves.

A huge bowl of pomegranates waited to be seeded. She'd have Demi scoop out each red pearl. Then she could shell the small mountain of pea pods.

If Euodia arrived to help today, she'd ask her to prepare the carrots and sauté the dates. Tomorrow Euodia should pickle the eggs.

"I'll braise the meat and bake the bread, and, of course, Euodia should make the hummus."

"I should what?"

Syntyche spun around, a smile lighting her face. “You’ve always made the best hummus in Philippi, maybe even Macedonia.”

“More lemon, less garlic, and a lot of tahini. Mater said it was more Hebrew than Greek.” She lifted one shoulder. “Anyone can make it.”

“Maybe, but you have it perfected.”

Euodia gave a quick nod, unclasped her palla, and placed it over a chair.

In the awkward silence, Demi bustled into the kitchen and edged along the wall. “I’m sorry to be late again, but I’ll stay and work longer. Are the pomegranates mine to husk?”

Without waiting for an answer, she scurried to the table.

“Euodia, this is Demi. Demi, our guest is my little sister, Euodia.”

Demi bobbed her head, glanced sideways and spoke without turning. “She’s beautiful, isn’t she?”

“She is.”

Euodia blushed. “What do you want done first?”

“I’ve decided that first you must…” Syntyche stopped herself. “Let me tell you what needs to be done, and you decide the order.”

Seeing her sister startle, she continued. “When I said I wanted you to forgive me, I should have added that I want to change. I’d like to work beside you, not over you. You are as capable in the kitchen as I am.”

“Mater taught us well.”

Their eyes met in a moment of remembrance and peace.

Euodia set the chickpeas to boil, chose a large mixing bowl, and began to juice lemons as Syntyche divided the dough into three thick strands for braiding.

"Demi, I can't stop in the middle of this, or I'll need to start over. Leave the pomegranates and take out that loaf of bread before it burns. Move quickly. My nose says it's ready."

Syntyche watched, puzzled, when Demi wiped her hands and moved backward toward the oven.

"What are you doing, Demi?"

"As you said."

"Walking backward? Look at me."

Demi turned slowly.

Syntyche gasped. "Your eye! What happened? Who struck you?"

"My uncle." Demi's shoulders slumped. "I only did as you said. He told me not to speak of it, but I told him again that he was in need of the Christ. And then he hit me." Fear shadowed her eyes. "Do I have to say it to him again?"

Euodia dropped the lemon and hurried to Demi's side. "Sit down. Let me see your eye. Did he knock you to the ground? Yes? Did you hit your head when you fell?"

She lifted Demi's chin. The swelling had already begun to darken. In a few weeks, the black eye would heal, but the cut on the lid concerned her. It needed treatment to avoid infection.

"This just happened, didn't it? Why didn't you tell us when you came in? Syntyche, I need a cold, wet cloth, and do you have comfrey?"

"What about my bread?"

Euodia thinned her lips, snatched a towel, yanked the bread from the oven, and slammed it on the table. She dipped a cloth in fresh water for Demi to hold against her eye.

Eyes cold, she repeated her question. "Comfrey?"

Syntyche pointed to her spice box. As the herb steeped, Euodia, trembling with defiance, turned on Syntyche.

"She is injured because of you and your insistence everyone be like you."

Bewildered, Syntyche stopped midbraid. "I only want—"

"For everyone to know the Lord Jesus. Yes, I understand that. I want it too, but not everyone wants to know Him."

"Well, they should."

Euodia turned away. "Demi, when the tea is very, very dark, I'll strain out the leaves and let it cool. It will help your eye heal. While it's steeping, go lie down on the other bed in Syntyche's room and keep that cold cloth on your eye."

"But…"

Syntyche nodded. "Do as she says, Demi. You'll still have a full day's wages."

With short, jerky motions, Euodia blended the tahini and lemon, peeled and chopped the garlic, and found the olive oil, salt, cumin, and paprika. All ingredients gathered in one spot, except for the chickpeas, which still had not softened, she left the kitchen.

Syntyche watched her leave. She must be going to check on Demi. Did Euodia feel strange walking through a house so familiar but no longer hers, to know its secrets, feel the same worn spots in the rugs, and see a memory in each corner? Did she remember their parents' voices as she passed the room that had been theirs?

Folding the dough first one direction and then the other, she wondered which folds of the past Euodia would remember. This house, which had held both laughter and loss, would either bring to mind comfort and closeness or dredge up hurt and resentment.

She shook her head to pull herself into the present. Last night's dreams, Demi's beaten face, and the tension pulsing between her and her sister disheartened her.

"Lord, what do You want from me?"

Unity.

She sank both hands into the dough and squeezed until it oozed between her fingers. "But I don't know how! How do I have unity and be true to who You made me? I don't want to lose my sister, but I don't want to lose me. God, is there a right answer? Do I have to choose?"

"Choose what, Syntyche?"

She must have spoken aloud. Euodia had returned, unnoticed, and watched her cautiously.

"Do I have to choose between being me and losing you, or losing me and having a sister?"

Sadness stretched across Euodia's face. "I don't know, Syntyche. I don't know." She tried to smile and failed. "At least we're in the same room and speaking."

Syntyche stretched out a dough-caked hand. "That's not enough for me. I miss you. I miss us. There has to be a way. I just don't know what it is."

Euodia gathered her palla. With a long, enigmatic look, she left the house.

The dough had dried and cracked before Syntyche moved. She scraped it off each finger and dug it from beneath her nails, wrapped it in a cloth, and disposed of it. That loaf would not have risen properly nor tasted good. It was full of grief and frustration and disappointment.

Hoping Euodia would return soon, she set the chickpeas to cool. No more bread baking today. The heaviness of her heart would find its way to her hands. Today was the day to mix vinegar and spices for a brine—sour, bitter ingredients like her thoughts.

Euodia shivered inside her light wool palla. She hadn't planned to walk. She'd instructed her driver to return late afternoon, but perhaps it was better to spend short times with Syntyche while their brokenness had such jagged edges.

What would it take to heal them?

A miracle! A wry smile lifted her lips. Yes, that should do it. She raised her gaze skyward. Good thing she knew a miracle worker.

She knew Syntyche was trying not to be overbearing and earnestly wanted to restore their relationship. But Syntyche would forever and always be—Syntyche. She'd seen her sister's bewilderment when confronted today.

She huddled in her palla and quickened her pace as a chill breeze swept through the streets. She glanced up at the darkening clouds. A rumble of thunder warned her that if she didn't hurry, she might be caught in a rain squall.

She looked up as the noise of a large carriage rolling through the streets drawing closer. A familiar carpentum with four matching horses approached from the opposite direction. Valeria. Stunningly arrayed in a full-sleeve stola that would hide any discoloration, the woman stared out the open window. Euodia lifted her hand in greeting only to hastily drop it when Valeria met her gaze and deliberately angled herself in the opposite direction.

Her steps lagged. With Valeria distancing herself, the other young matrons would follow her lead. The loss of their friendship—if it could truly be called that—did not sting as much as the growing isolation. Severed from the elite and scorned by her church, she felt her world shrinking. Isolated, she could not serve.

Head drooping, she relived the day she'd assured Valeria she did not have leprosy. Was the coldness from vulnerability as she first thought, or was it her claim to be a Christ follower?

Possible but not probable, Amelia may have sent word to disassociate with her, even knowing it would affect Marcellus.

"Am I of no use to anyone anymore?"

From behind her, a carriage rumbled to a stop amid the clatter of hooves. Large drops of rain splayed dirt when they hit the marble pavers.

"Get in."

Valeria motioned for her to hurry. Euodia gathered her skirts and stepped inside.

Thunder bellowed across the city as the unseasonable downpour released its fury. It was no match for the anger in Valeria's face or her low growl.

"I warned you to say nothing."

Euodia did not pretend to misunderstand. "She already knew." Amelia's horror of learning she'd been in Valeria's house had been genuine.

Shock raced across Valeria's face. "I told no one but you. No one."

"Except the priests of every temple—Egyptian, Roman, Greek—who took your bribes to say nothing."

"You took my bribe for your Hebrew God?"

"Yes, and sent it to be used to bring comfort to those in need—not to be hoarded or to pay for my silence."

Valeria drummed her perfectly manicured fingernails against her silk-clad arm before pointing one jeweled finger at Euodia. "You're one of those traitors who won't worship Nero."

"I'm a Christ follower. If that makes me a traitor, then tell your driver to stop. I'll walk the rest of the way and never bother you again even with a greeting. Valeria, believe me. I want nothing from you."

Valeria scrutinized her before allowing her face and voice to soften. "I don't know what to think about you, but I can't be seen with a follower of that Jew. He's a God for peasants."

She ran a finger along the inside of an emerald-eyed snake bracelet. "I'm watched constantly because of my family connections, now more than ever because of the leprosy rumors. You are no longer an asset to me even if your husband is a patrician and a great artist. I will not tell Cousin Nero, but if he ever heard the wife of Marcellus Atticus Cassius was a Christ follower, it would be the end of your husband's career."

Shocked, Euodia remained speechless. Her faith could truly harm Marcellus? He was not being overly cautious? If Valeria knew Marcellus was also a believer, would she remain silent?

The carriage stopped at the entrance to her house. She disembarked and mounted the steps to her home. Uncertain if she'd thanked Valeria for the ride and for her promise of silence, she turned, but the carriage had been driven away. Standing in the rain, drenched and numb, Euodia understood how Linus must feel during a bath—as if someone emptied the slop bucket on his head.

Inside, she let Claudia and Doris take her dripping palla, light the braziers, and usher her into a steaming bath. Doris left with a message for Cook to warm soup and bread.

"You had a guest today, mistress." Claudia squeezed water from Euodia's sopping hair.

"Oh?" Euodia gave silent thanks for having missed whoever it was. Syntyche and Valeria were enough for one day.

"She's been here before. Wears a lot of perfume and bracelets, likes purple."

"Malitta."

"Yes. She said she'd call again later this week."

Surprised, Euodia did not respond. There had been no other message from Malitta since she'd accompanied her home after that awful day. She too must have decided not to associate with her, or Malitta had learned of Tymon's insistence Euodia not befriend her. Servants talked, even hers, as hard as she'd worked to earn their loyalty with her kindness. It was too much to think of tonight.

She yawned. "I'll be with my sister for the next few days." If it was urgent, Malitta could find her in Syntyche's kitchen. Maybe she'd put her to work. Only five days remained to prepare for the feast.

Sleep had almost claimed her when two of Valeria's words startled her to complete awareness. "Cousin Nero." If Nero could kill his own mater, what would he do to Marcellus?

"Syneeeeee!"

Ty's unexpected roar of her name caused Syntyche to choke on her morning tea. Gasping for breath, she grabbed a cloth and stumbled out of the kitchen while dabbing at the stain on her fresh stola.

She halted just inside his office. "Ty, are you hurt? What's happened?"

"You tell me."

Lifting her hands in frustration, she spun in a circle searching the room for a catastrophe. Seeing nothing, she pivoted back to him. "What?"

"The steward tells me my home has become a bakery, a storehouse, a themopolium for your Jesus people. I warned you when you first moved in here there would be none of those people here."

Syntyche jammed her hands on her hips. "That's the reason for all your noise?" She held up a finger to still his protests. "First, it is not a thermopolium. I serve no one any food or drink in your house. Second, 'those' people are not coming here. Third, Euodia and I are preparing a feast—one single meal—for 'those' people who will *not* be eating it here. And fourth, the supplies were paid for by an anonymous donor, so except for a bit of salt, it's not costing you anything."

"You and Euodia? You're working together? In this house?"

"She's making the hummus." Syntyche prayed she'd return to finish it. "Do you want her to replace the salt she used without asking you?"

If she were less brave, she'd wilt before his glare.

"Don't be ridiculous."

"Exactly what is your concern, Ty? Goodness, you sounded like a wounded lion I saw at a beast show in the arena."

"Beast show? You patronize that spectacle that makes a mockery of those magnificent creatures? Those shows are why lions can hardly be found in Macedonia. They've all been captured and sent to Rome and—"

"Distraction doesn't work with me either, dear brother. Have you finished scaring years off my life with your roars?"

Ty glared at her then lowered his eyes and dropped onto the chair behind his desk. "Asking instead of accusing would have been better. I'm sorry." He pinched the bridge of his nose.

She sat on the edge of a chair. "What really bothers you, Ty? Do you want us to cook elsewhere? It's almost over. The feast—um—meal is in five days. It only happens once a year."

"I hesitate to tell you."

"Because?"

"I do not want you to lecture me about your God. If I tell you, not a word about Him. Agreed?"

Curious, she nodded and leaned forward.

"I received a letter from Marcus."

"Your friend deceived by—"

"Don't say her name in this house."

Syntyche held up her palms in surrender. "As you will. Don't snap at me. Is all well with him?"

Ty crossed his arms and again rubbed the bridge of his nose. "He wrote that he regrets his long silence, that he never blamed me for…her, but it was too painful an experience to think about, and driving it from his thoughts meant having no contact with anyone in Philippi."

"Ty, that's wonderful. It makes sense, and what relief you must feel."

Ty appeared more disgruntled than relieved. "Yes, of course I do. He is a good man—one I respect enormously. I'm glad he still considers me a friend."

"What caused him to write after all this time?"

Ty stared into the distance then enunciated as if the words were unfamiliar—a tongue as different as those in Germania. "He asked if I'd send him the address of…her. He decided he must forgive…her."

"You mean Mal..."

At his narrowed eyes, she swallowed the name and smiled brightly. "Marvelous—and gracious, especially as deeply as she wounded him." She shook her head, amazed. "What prompted it, do you suppose?"

"Not a word, Synee. You promised."

She crossed both hands over her lips to assure him she'd not speak.

Ty worked his mouth as if it held a bitter olive he could not expel. "He said he is compelled to forgive others so that he might be forgiven."

Eyes locked on his, riveted by his words, she strained to hear what he ground out.

"Marcus writes he is a Christ follower." Ty dropped his head in his hands. "He met a man named Paul, who appealed to his intellect and led him to faith."

A gasp escaped in spite of her precautions. Blinking, mind racing, she glimpsed the Lord's hand touching Ty's life.

He lifted his head. "Could it be the same Paul you know?"

"Yes." Tears of gratitude flooded her eyes. The Lord was redeeming her failures through the witness of Paul—yet in a Roman prison—to reach her brother in Philippi. Marcus's words once carried more weight with Ty than anyone she knew.

"I'm so disappointed in him."

The chills she felt hearing of Marcus's faith turned to ice in her veins. She'd promised not to speak. Now, she could not. Lowering her hands, she waited for him to continue speaking.

"Synee, people do not die and come back to life. Even a child understands that. I don't know how this Jesus has managed to persuade intelligent, educated thinkers otherwise."

Lord?

Patience.

No direction from Him could have been more difficult to obey.

Ty rubbed his neck with a deep sigh. "How could Marcus have let himself be deceived? What would your Paul have said to him? I need to understand, so tell me."

"Ty, you know in Athens, there is an altar to the unknown god?"

"Yes, and I know the story of the sheep."

Syntyche cocked her head. "What sheep?"

"Really, Synee?"

She shrugged. "No idea."

"Fine, short version. Five or six hundred years ago, a plague struck Athens. No cure, no end in sight, no explanation other than a god needed appeasing."

"Which one?"

"Exactly. Athens has hundreds of gods. City leaders called in a man named Epimenides—you really don't know this story? He determined all the known gods of Athens had been placated and there was an unknown god causing the plague."

"I don't think—"

"Wait. Epimenides ordered a flock of hungry sheep be loosed on Areopagus—Mars Hill is what the Romans call it—and proclaimed that any sheep that lay down and did not eat was to be sacrificed at that spot and an altar built to the unknown god."

"That makes no sense."

"Right. Like a dead man returning to life. So, several sheep lay down, several altars were built, and—boom—the plague stopped. Through the centuries, all but one of the altars to the unknown gods were lost to time or decay. There's your sheep story."

"And your answer, Ty. Hundreds of years ago, even with all our gods, we were still searching for truth. We sensed we were missing something, so we had an altar with no idol, no description of a god."

"Tell me you do not believe the nonsense of the story."

"Honestly, I can imagine our ancestors doing that. Do not raise your eyebrows at me. I'm trying to explain what Paul may have said to Marcus."

"I'm listening."

"First, he realized Marcus was searching for truth. Then he explained that the Lord is a God of mercy and comfort, forgiveness, and healing. He might have—"

"Enough."

"You asked."

"I did. I've decided to write Marcus and learn exactly what Paul told him. Then I can help him see how he was deceived. Synee, he's in danger. He's in Rome, under the emperor's nose—an emperor who, more than any others, expects to be worshiped as part of the Imperial cult. If I can persuade him to see reason, it might save his life."

When Ty began gathering parchment and a pen, Syntyche understood she was dismissed. She sauntered to the kitchen, smiling. Ty didn't realize it, but he'd opened the door to hearing more about her Lord.

Entering the kitchen, she smiled broadly. Euodia had returned to help.

"Euodia! You came back. I'm so glad."

Her sister made a noncommittal sound. A greeting? Or groan from straining to carry a large pot of boiled eggs to the table?

Syntyche set water to boil, turned the meat in its marinade and gathered the ingredients for more challah. As much as was needed for the feast, it was a good thing she liked to bake.

Euodia must have arrived not long after Ty bellowed. The skins from the chickpeas had been removed, and she'd begun to mash the softened beans.

"I didn't expect you this early or I'd have set everything up for you. Not much has changed since we both lived here, but I did rearrange a few things."

The scraping, kneading rhythm of a kitchen with its fire crackles and bubbling water softened the silence between them. Syntyche hummed softly. Ty would come to faith, and peace with Euodia seemed possible.

"Syntyche, do you ever wonder what your faith could cost you? Are you ever afraid?"

Fear sharp as a labor pain stilled her hands. Panic swelled, crested, ebbed, until she could again breathe, again pretend its presence never consumed her, again deny it lurked deep within.

"I saw Valeria yesterday. Her carpentum passed just as the rain began and she had her driver take me home. She said Marcellus could be in danger because I'm a Christ follower. If she knew he is too, she might tell Nero. He's her cousin." Her voice broke. "Syntyche, I'm so scared."

At Euodia's plaintive tone, Syntyche shoved her own feelings into the recesses of her being. So seldom did terror find release, she lived refusing to admit its existence.

She fought the urge to draw her little sister close and comfort her with whatever she needed to hear, that Valeria was mistaken, that nothing bad would happen, that everything was fine. Instead, she retreated behind her pride.

"No. Fear would cripple me. I forbid it in my life and so should you."

Euodia drooped.

Syntyche glanced at her sister's forlorn profile. Confessing weakness to Euodia meant the end of denial—acknowledging it to herself—and the Lord, who already knew. It risked Euodia seeing her differently, seeing herself differently, a different relationship. Stronger? Weaker? A loss of influence? A new beginning?

Faith carried a cost. So did love. Sometimes the cost was too high.

"You're right, Syntyche. I should be more like you."

The resignation in her voice warned Syntyche that the hummus would taste more bitter than usual. The thoughts of a cook were revealed in her food.

Heavy footsteps announced Ty's approach. The smile he wore on entering the kitchen faded as if he sensed the tension between his sisters.

"Euodia. Welcome. It's good to see you here. Use all the salt you need."

She cocked her head, puzzlement written on her face.

"Never mind." He colored. "It was a misunderstanding. Synee, I'll be home early evening. I'm taking the letter to the Neapolis port instead of sending it overland. It's urgent Marcus receive it quickly."

Euodia stirred salt into the hummus. "Marcus? Your friend?"

"Synee will tell you."

Before she could stop him, Marcus broke a challah loaf in half. "This is good, Synee. I had one yesterday too, since there were several. They're soft, almost sweet. Make these more often."

He scooped challah through the bowl of hummus, leaving a wide channel, and bit off a large chunk. Mouth full, he took half the loaf and left.

The sisters stared at his retreating back then at each other. Tentative grins and then a burst of laughter sweetened the room.

"It's a good thing you like to bake, Synee."

"I do, but can we hide the food at your house? I'm running out of time with it only a few days away."

"Cook is a warrior when it comes to guarding food. She'll not let anyone, even Marcellus, steal a bite. We'll load up the carriage when it returns for me." Euodia glanced around the room. "Where's Demi?"

"I told her to stay home and rest." A quest for affirmation wrinkled Syntyche's brow. "And not to say another word about our Lord to her uncle unless he asked."

She squirmed guiltily beneath the warmth in Euodia's eyes. She'd lied to her sister about being fearless. The cold distance would reappear when she confessed. She opened her mouth to admit her falsehood then closed it. She'd bask in the warmth for a while before it disappeared forever.

CHAPTER TWENTY-TWO

The next day, the sisters squeezed into Euodia's carriage. They'd filled it with loaves of bread, the freshly roasted meat, and five dozen pickled eggs still in their beet or turmeric brine. The bowls of hummus sat secure on their laps or between their feet.

Euodia relaxed into the familiar comfort of being next to her stubborn, fearless sister. Encouraged by Syntyche's softened stance toward Demi, maybe she too could change, become more outspoken. Neither of them was wrong. They needed to meet in the middle. She ignored the unease rippling through her spirit at the thought.

The carpentum braked and lurched. She tightened her arms around the bowl. At least if the hummus spilled, she wouldn't be dyed red or yellow like the eggs in their brine.

Pastels tinted the September twilight. The pleasant warmth of the day was dropping quickly as the sun sought its well-earned rest. She thought wistfully of the comfort of her bed. She'd sleep well tonight unless Linus whined to go out before morning.

The carriage stopped, and Euodia clambered out, ran up the steps, and called for Claudia.

Claudia hurried forward, looking apologetic.

"I'm sorry, mistress. She pushed past Felix and wouldn't leave."

Euodia frowned not seeing anyone. "Who?"

"That purple woman. She's in the master's studio."

Enough. Helena once and Malitta twice. When her husband returned, she'd insist they hire a guard who could not be overrun by a single woman. It was disconcerting to have someone appear in her bedroom as Malitta had, but to enter Marcellus's private studio? He allowed no one in his studio, not even her. *Livid* would not begin to describe his anger if he returned home unexpectedly and discovered her invasion.

"Syntyche is outside with food for Cook to guard. See it is brought in, and tell my sister I will see her tomorrow. Have the carriage drive her home. I'll attend to our guest."

Euodia walked decisively to his studio. Malitta stood, bangled wrists crossed behind her back, perusing Marcellus's artwork.

"He's immensely talented."

"I think so. Malitta, come to the garden with me. I'll send for refreshments."

"No. The mosquitos are out in droves."

The mosquitos had almost disappeared by this time of year, but Euodia didn't argue.

"Then come to the dining room with me so we can sit and visit."

Malitta turned. "You look better. I've never seen anyone as overwrought as you were that day. It's a shame you had to suffer for your sister's behavior."

A headache began its slow drumming. "I'm glad you're here, Malitta. I'm indebted to you for staying with me and helping me home. I need you to understand that I didn't suffer for my sister's actions. Mine, though different from Syntyche's, were as harmful as hers."

Malitta shrugged. "Whatever brings you comfort. I've never heard you speak against anyone or anything or push your beliefs on another."

"That might be the problem."

Malitta startled, and Euodia hastened to explain. "Not that I should speak against someone, but there are times I should speak up for someone."

Malitta waved her hand in dismissal. A ripple of aged perfume wafted forward. If Marcellus returned, he'd know someone had been in here. The room reeked of rancid musk.

"Please, Malitta, permit me to escort you to a more comfortable room."

When she ushered Malitta out of the studio, Euodia's relief vanished. Syntyche waited for her in the atrium.

She closed her eyes, seeking strength. Claudia and Doris hovered in the background. How her sister—known to be a Christ follower—reacted to Malitta, would be whispered throughout the city.

Tension ricocheted between her guest and her sister, leaving Euodia as wilted as if she stood in the breathless heat and humidity of a sluggish August night. The two women appraised each other—gladiators in a ring. Every diplomatic tactic she'd known fled from her mind, along with every thought. Only one word remained that she could call forth.

Lord?

See.

See what? A battlefield? A bloodbath? A disaster? Two women—once friends—who no longer shared anything except mutual dislike. Strong women who were nothing alike. Women who cared about Ty. Women she cared about. What was she supposed to see?

Insight ripped through her, the clarity of its force shocking, devastating. Stunned, she grasped what she'd been shown.

Herself. Her sister. At war. Comparing. Criticizing. Judging.

This is how she and Syntyche appeared to others. No wonder they'd become pariahs instead of leaders. No wonder Ty rejected their witness of the Lord. No wonder Paul publicly and permanently corrected them. Untreated wounds spread their infection until the entire body was affected.

Although healing had begun for her and her sister, they needed to be forgiven by others who'd suffered from their behavior.

"Synee, while I speak with my guest, please, would you direct and advise Cook of our dilemma? She'll need your input and guidance on what to store where."

"Malitta, thank you for waiting. It's urgent I speak with you."

She led her to a small room furnished with only two chairs and a low table. Malitta perched on the edge of her seat as if preparing to escape. Euodia reached for her hand.

"Malitta, you have been so kind to me, standing beside me when I felt alone. You are one of the few who did not abandon me."

Malitta preened beneath the compliment.

"Therefore, I come to you first, before anyone else, asking for your forgiveness. You should never have been in the compromising situations I placed you in. There is no excuse except my pride and selfishness for you to have been subjected to what is not Christlike behavior. You have not made a decision to trust my Lord, but I beg you to give me another chance to show how He changes people."

Malitta regarded her as if weighing each word and searching for criticism.

"There is more I must confess. Ty told me of your childhood friendship and how it was destroyed."

Malitta pulled her hand away.

"Just as I know my Lord will forgive my misdeeds, I know He will forgive you for any hurt or harm you have caused others. He is mercy."

Malitta stood. Drawing herself to her full height, she looked down her regal nose at Euodia.

"I do not need mercy nor forgiveness nor your Lord."

She stalked out of the room. Euodia heard the front door slam.

Lord?

Joy.

Syntyche's flat-footed steps neared. Her sister drew her to her feet and wrapped her arms around her in an unshakeable sister hug.

"I heard. I'm so proud of you."

Joy.

CHAPTER TWENTY-THREE

Sleep refused to release Euodia from the day's revelation. Each twist and turn brought to mind another person she needed to ask for forgiveness—even Linus, since he'd jumped to the floor during her restlessness.

Clement, Syzygus, Paul, the women of the church, Tymon, her servants, the poor who'd witnessed her tirade against Syntyche… She pulled the bedcover over her head, wishing to hide.

"Lord, where do I start?"

Helena.

Foreboding like the distant rumble of thunder rolled through her. Was the relationship irreparable? Was Helena so offended there was no hope? Unsettled, she decided to send Synee word that she'd be late in the morning.

Would her sister go with her? She curled into a ball. It was not right to ask someone else to do what she needed to do. Syntyche's journey of healing was between her and the Lord, although maybe together they could write Paul a letter of remorse for the trouble they'd caused.

Not a lot of time remained before the feast of new beginnings. How glorious a new beginning sounded, to start with a clean conscience, assured she'd done all she could to be forgiven. Never again would she be the cause of dissent within the fellowship of believers.

Euodia snapped her fingers. Linus ran to her arms for a snuggle and scratch. Would everyone be as quick to forgive?

She dressed with care, choosing a stola to serve for both the visit and kitchen work. After entrusting Linus to the kitchen boy's care, she refused Cook's offer of food and requested the small carriage be brought to the front. It would be quicker to ride than walk today. Helena woke while it was still dark. She'd not mind an early visitor.

Asking forgiveness was the right thing to do. A dry mouth, clammy hands, and quivering legs would not stop her. Nothing would.

Euodia stood in the atrium of Helena's house, unwilling to assume she was welcome to sit in comfort while Helena decided whether or not to see her. After a bit, she shifted her weight. Helena must be in no hurry to speak with her. She'd been wrong to arrive uninvited and so early. Sending a messenger with a request to visit would have been better.

Footsteps alerted her that someone approached. A disheveled Clement did not speak but motioned her to follow him.

"Brother Clement, I'm sorry. I should not have arrived unannounced. I was eager to apologize to you and Helena and did not think clearly."

His continued silence confused her.

"I can leave and return another time."

He shook his head and motioned her to enter Helena's room ahead of him. The frail woman's eyes were closed, her skin the color of the bleached linen sheets.

"It is good you came when you did, Euodia. I believe it will not be much longer until she joins our Lord."

Euodia crossed to the bed, searching for a slight movement—assurance Helena still lived. Long seconds passed before another breath eased through the still body. She turned to Clement. He nodded.

"I know. I've been with her all night."

"I'm so sorry. I'll leave."

"Stay. She'd want you here."

Euodia knelt by the bed. Gingerly, she cradled Helena's delicate hand.

"Dearest friend, I've come to beg your forgiveness. You are more than a faithful friend, more than a sister in Christ. You are the mater I lost and longed for even when I turned away from you. You, dear lady, are a truth speaker, and knowing you, I know my Lord better. He shines in you."

She pressed her lips to the pale forehead and swept back a silver-white strand of hair. Clement moved to the other side of the bed. His hand cupped his mater's thin shoulder. Together they counted the seconds between her shallow breaths until... Still, they waited in hopeless hope for one more breath, for a sign she remained this side of the veil.

The lifeless hands grew cold, their death chill seeping beneath Euodia's skin. Her gaze caressed the dear face. Tears would flow later—tears for her loss, for the wasted time, for the sorrow she'd caused this woman.

Seated by the deathbed, Euodia thanked God He'd sent her here first and for the privilege of knowing and loving Helena. Never again would pride keep her from the ones she loved.

Syntyche cocked her head, listening for the sound of Euodia's carriage. The little servant girl said Euodia would be late, but this late? Did her sister understand how much they had to do?

One remaining day to finish cooking and baking. Syntyche mentally listed each remaining task. Sautéing the dates would be the final dish, and that was for Euodia to accomplish.

Tomorrow was the feast. Tomorrow she faced the church she'd harmed. Did acceptance and forgiveness await, or would her apologies be rejected?

She balanced an empty bowl on her knees and reached for a bunch of kale—such a bitter green unless you knew its wonderful secret. She folded a leaf and tore it from the stem. Her secret was not wonderful, and tomorrow everyone would hear it.

Dread slowed her hands. Recognizing Pride and its sister, Comparison, in herself was painful. Confessing it in public—excruciating. But if that was what it took to show her repentance, that was what she'd do.

Leaf by leaf she stripped out the stiff stem. If the stem remained, the kale would be too tough to be palatable.

"Lord, slay my pride. Strip it from me."

After discarding the stems, she washed the kale, cleaning the sand and dirt that clung to the leaves.

"And wash me of the dirt that clings."

The bowl of clean greens on her lap, she tore each leaf into small pieces.

Only a few steps remained to sweeten and soften the kale—to sweeten and soften her.

She added a bit of olive oil and massaged the leaves, squeezing and bruising them until the leaves darkened and became fragrant. Finally, she added salt and lemon juice.

Syntyche contemplated the shining emerald greens. They'd been stripped, torn and bruised, ready to bring strength and healing.

"Lord, through Your hand on me, bring strength and healing."

A gust of wind through the door broke into her thoughts. Euodia stood in the entrance.

Syntyche held up a handful of crushed greens. "Euodia, it's the kale. I'm like the kale that needed to be..." Her sister's pallor halted her words.

Euodia's lips barely moved. "Synee, it's Helena."

Syntyche pushed the bowl onto the table and hurried across the room to pull out a chair. "Sit before you fall. What happened?"

Euodia wrapped herself in her arms. "She's gone."

"Gone where?" Understanding dawned. "Oh. Oh no. When? I didn't know she was ill."

"This morning. I went to apologize, to make peace, and while I was there, she…left."

"Clement?"

"Exhausted but peaceful. He knows his grief is temporary."

"What can we do?"

Euodia shook her head. "Nothing. He sent for Brother Syzygus. I'm not sure, but I think we can do nothing more until fellowship has been restored."

"Did she suffer?"

Euodia shook her head. "I don't think so. She looked serene, almost content."

"I wish you could have talked to Helena before she passed."

Euodia dabbed at the tears pooling in her eyes. "I did. She heard me, though she didn't say anything or even squeeze my hand. The Lord nudged me to see her first thing this morning. It was as if she waited for us to be at peace before she left." She closed her eyes before speaking again.

"I've never been present at a death like hers. There was peace and light and the strangest sense of joy. I'm glad she's with the Lord and sorry for me. I've lost such a friend. Synee, can you crack and bleed inside? It's as if something has been torn away and can't be replaced."

Syntyche's eyes filled. "That is my every day, missing Alex and Lily."

"How do you keep going?"

"There's not an easy answer or a single answer. Faith. Prayer. Crying myself to sleep. Being thankful I loved and was loved. Each day is different and a different facet of grief.

Sometimes it is a subtle ache. Other times it is a wave that drowns me."

"I never knew. You're always so strong."

"Not really." Syntyche took a deep breath. "There's more. This is not the best time. It might be the worst possible time, but there's something I need to tell you. I lied to you." She ached at the subtle shuttering of Euodia's eyes.

"You asked if I ever wonder what my faith might cost me. I do. I'm terrified, not fearless. Will I be arrested again, flogged this time? Will I lose Ty? If the Roman government sees me as a troublemaker instead of just a nuisance to a grumpy merchant, I could be killed or exiled. Will I remain faithful no matter what?"

Syntyche rubbed her forehead and eyes as if to erase the images. "Your fear for Marcellus is realistic, and I do not trust Valeria's discretion. Forgive me for dismissing your concerns. It was unkind. However, I also spoke truth to you. Fear will not cripple me or define me."

Euodia folded her arms on the table and rested her head on them.

Syntyche reached across the table and patted Euodia's arm. "I'm sorry. You're grieving for Helena, and now you're worried about me and Marcellus. I should have waited to tell you, but I wanted us to have a fresh start too." She brushed aside the hair that had fallen across Euodia's face. "I understand what Brother Aaron said about the Jews feeling an awesome responsibility to repent and atone. These ten days have filled me with fear and wonder—with awe—as I try to right the relationships I've skewed."

"You were right to tell me." Euodia's muffled voice sounded tired. "I want things to be different between us, Synee. I'm not sure where to start."

"Speaking truth with gentleness is where I'm beginning."

Euodia propped her head higher, fisting her hands to support her chin. "I'm going to let you be you and me be me, not compare us and decide one of us is better than the other."

"Starting now."

"Now."

Syntyche gestured to the bowl of kale. "First decision in working together is what will we do with all this food since the feast is canceled?"

"As I was leaving, Clement said to tell you he still planned it for tomorrow."

"No. That will be too hard on him. He wasn't thinking clearly."

"He insisted—said he would not dismiss all your work and that it will be a celebration of his mater's new life with our Lord as well as new beginnings for our church."

Syntyche covered her mouth. "He thought of me in his grief?"

"Synee, he's a good man. I believe he thinks of you a lot."

"Did I tell you we talked, and he forgave me for the difficulties I caused?"

Euodia did not answer, but her eyes grew anxious. "Synee, where will we have the feast? No matter what Clement says, it cannot be at his home. Their servants will be mourning Helena. It wouldn't be right to add this burden to them." She hesitated. "It could be held at my house."

"We'll have it here. I know you're anxious for Marcellus after Valeria's comments."

"But Tymon..."

"Isn't here for me to ask. He left early this morning for a few days. It will all be over when he returns." Her voice softened. "If he knew the circumstances, I think he'd agree. And if he doesn't understand, I'll be moving in with you and bringing Demi. Cook will have to learn to share her kitchen."

Euodia fidgeted with her clothes. "Synee, tomorrow is the day."

"Yes, the feast. We are ready except for what can only be done at the last moment." She looked closer. "You are worried about tomorrow."

"It is the first day back at worship since..."

"Since Paul's letter." Syntyche reached in the bowl and shredded a piece of kale. "I dread going. Clement said he'd allow us to speak if we chose to."

Euodia gulped. "I wouldn't know what to say."

"'I'm sorry. Please forgive me.' What else is there?"

"And if they turn their backs on us? Synee, that would be unbearable."

"Then they are guilty of hard hearts. Euodia, everyone in the world has made mistakes that hurt other people. Everyone has regrets. Everyone needs forgiveness."

"I suppose, but not everyone has to ask for it in public."

"Nor do you. I am more at fault than you, and I will stand before all and admit it."

Euodia's look stopped her.

"Synee, our wrong is equal. It's been different for each of us, but we've both compared and judged each other and others, like Amelia and Valeria and—"

"Malitta." Syntyche groaned. "I not only judged her but spoke harshly to her too."

"I doubt she will be there tomorrow when we apologize to the believers."

"Brother Aaron said we needed to restore relationship between anyone we wronged, even nonbelievers. We only have tonight left in the Days of Awe."

"When we finish here, I'll go with you, Synee. I judged her too, not out loud but in my thoughts."

Demi bounced into the house. "Syntyche, we're back from the delivery. Your sister's driver is ready to take her home."

Syntyche couldn't help smiling at the girl's excitement. It wasn't often she rode in an elaborate carriage. "All went smoothly?"

"Clement's cook was relieved to have less cooking to do and said to thank you for sending food for the guests. A lot of people were there to grieve with him in the loss of his mater."

"Demi, Euodia and I have a visit we must make this afternoon even though it is late. I want you to put these last dishes and pans to soak and put away as much as you can before you go home. If you'd like, take some food to your uncle."

Syntyche tied her sandals and picked up the palla she'd brought in to the room. "Euodia, do you know Malitta's address?"

"No, but the driver may recognize the name."

When Euodia asked if he could take them to the home of Draco Spurius and his eyes lit up, Syntyche knew it would be a magnificent dwelling.

"Synee, should we take a gift of food, a peace offering?"

"Yes." Syntyche unfolded a cloth and then crumpled it, leaving it on the table. "No. We are taking our offenses and unfairness and offering apologies to her. Let her decision to forgive us or to dismiss our remorse be based on her feelings, not on a bribe."

"As you wish. Ready?"

Syntyche followed her out of the house and climbed in the carriage after Euodia. The driver snapped the reins, and the carriage lurched forward.

Malitta's house sat higher on the mountain than Valeria's house. Massive doors, flanked by guards, barred a casual entrance. The woman had married into wealth even if she'd not won the titled Marcus.

Why would Malitta have any interest in revenge against Ty when she'd not suffered financially and confessed to have been using Marcus? Syntyche puzzled the woman's motives, unable to find the key.

She gave the guard her name. When he returned, they were led into an atrium almost as large as Clement's entire house. Spaced along the pool, urns overflowing with greenery gave the sense they'd entered a garden. Purple and lavender silk pillows cushioned the sofa lining the wall. Syntyche sank into their softness and fingered the silk. The smooth, almost waxy feeling revealed its high quality. She could still see Pater's eyes shining when he told her fine silk seemed to move as if it were alive.

Euodia's whisper drew her back to the present. "How long do you think she'll make us wait?"

"I don't care. Touch this silk and look at the murals and the mosaics. I'll gladly sit here all night."

An hour later, Syntyche wondered if Malitta had overheard and was testing her determination. She'd studied the drape of the plants, the colors of the mosaics and the stories of the murals. She wiggled uncomfortably. The day had begun early, and she'd been standing most of it. Her feet ached.

Euodia was dozing, her head on Syntyche's shoulder, when a servant summoned them to Malitta's presence. She nudged her sister awake and stood, gingerly placing weight on her swelling feet. Arm in arm, Euodia yawning, they followed the servant past a picture gallery and another room of statues and busts until the girl stopped and motioned for them to enter.

They stepped onto a beautifully patterned rug woven with silver threads. Malitta reclined on a delicate sofa with gilded legs and silver cushions. Beside her, an intricately carved ivory table held a glass chalice.

They stood, feet sinking into the rug's thickness, waiting for Malitta to speak.

"What brings you here?"

The crispness of her voice belied interest, but the wariness in her eyes and the inward pull and rigid set of her shoulders revealed her tension.

Syntyche cleared her throat, but before she could begin, Euodia spoke.

"Malitta, thank you for seeing us."

"I'm not giving any more money."

"I would never ask for any, but Syntyche and I have come here to ask something of you, something only you can give us."

"As I suspected."

Euodia stepped forward.

Malitta tensed. "I have guards everywhere in this house."

"Oh, Malitta, we did not come here to cause harm."

"Then why? To remind me how I've hurt others?"

"No. Never again." Tears laced Euodia's voice. "We are here to tell you we realize we have hurt you and to apologize, to ask your forgiveness."

Malitta blinked.

Cautiously, Syntyche inched forward to stand beside Euodia. "I'm sorry, Malitta. I have spoken to you in anger and with disrespect. I accepted Ty's opinion of you without question and without hearing your truth. Worse still, I compared you to me and judged you as less than me. You are not."

Syntyche dared another step forward. "Malitta, you have done no worse than I."

"Nor I." Euodia stretched out her hand. "Nor Brother Clement nor Helena. In the eyes of our Lord, we have all sinned and need forgiveness from Him."

Malitta's gaze darted between them as if searching for a snare.

Syntyche raised her hands, palms upward. "We are not here to tell you of our Lord. We are here to beg your forgiveness because He has shown us we wronged you—many times."

Euodia dashed a tear from her face. "Will you forgive us?"

"Please?"

"Does your brother know you have come here?" Her query was stiff, accusatory. "He warned me to stay away from you."

"He does not know." Syntyche placed a hand over her heart. "If you wish it, he never will. This is between us. It has nothing to do with him."

Malitta breathed deeply. Her shoulders eased downward. "I don't know what to say."

"You do not need to say anything." Syntyche hoped Malitta heard her earnestness. "We will not bother you again. Forgiveness is a gift we do not deserve, and we will not badger you for it, nor do we want you to think you must grant it."

Euodia swayed, and Syntyche caught her around the waist as her knees buckled.

"I'm fine, just a bit dizzy."

Malitta swung off the sofa and clapped her hands. Three servants soundlessly appeared. "Chairs, water, and food for my"—she darted a look at them—"friends?"

Syntyche closed her eyes in relief. "Friends. Are we forgiven?"

"Yes. Am I?"

"By us, yes." Syntyche hesitated. "Do you want to hear more? I'm learning to ask instead of charging ahead like a runaway horse."

Together they ushered Euodia to the sofa and gently pushed her to sit. Malitta lifted Euodia's knees onto the sofa, ignoring her protests.

"She's had a long day. Sister Helena died this morning. They were very close friends."

"Helena was always kind to me. I'm not sure she liked me, but she was kind." Malitta smoothed the silk of her stola. "I don't understand what Paul meant when he admonished you to be of the same mind."

Syntyche winked at Euodia. "We had trouble understanding it too, but I think we have finally grasped it. Brother Clement helped me see the truth."

"Brother Syzygus and…" Euodia blinked away tears. "Helena helped me."

Syntyche nodded at Euodia. "There is not a right way or a wrong way to share the story of our Lord. I thought my bold way was more effective, and Euodia thought her gentle way was better."

"What's needed is both ways. We are of one mind in that we both want everyone to know Him. We are of one mind by accepting that each of us has a different part—but of equal value—in sharing. I want to honor Euodia's service to others, and I think she's more appreciative of my directness."

Euodia nodded. "When I stopped comparing myself to her, I stopped judging her."

"And when I stopped judging Euodia, I saw so much to appreciate about the way she interacts with people."

"I knew something was different between the two of you." Malitta pointed to the table where food and drink had been set.

"Please, have something to eat and then, if you have time, yes, I want to hear your story, not what Clement and Syzygus say."

"I will always make time." Syntyche took a deep breath. "Darkness covered the souls of all people. Fathomless darkness...the darkness of comparison and judgment and pride. I too lived in that murkiness, unaware there was a different way to live and that the Creator of all had created a way to escape the hopelessness and bring light into life."

She bit her lip. "When my husband and child died, the grief would have overwhelmed and smothered me if He hadn't walked through the sorrow by my side. He was already my Savior, forgiving me of my sins, but He became more. He is the lifter of my head, the guide of my life, and when I allow it, the harness on my tongue." Her eyes twinkled. "As you know, a harness is badly needed."

Malitta's eyes crinkled in laughter.

Euodia roused herself to sit upright. "He has gifted each of us differently so we may tell others about Him, but Synee and I forgot that, and as you realize, caused a lot of trouble for others. Malitta, what amazes me is He continues to forgive, no matter how often we forget to look to Him for guidance and instead put ourselves first."

Lines creased Malitta's forehead. "There's so much I wish I could change. You have no idea the lies I've told you two or the ways I've hurt your church. I was angry at Marcus and jealous of you both—you seem so 'good.'" She smiled wryly. "Most of my life needs to be forgiven, and there's no possibility of righting the wrongs."

Syntyche reached for her hand. "This is what I do. I take one regret and turn it over to Him, then another and another."

"I'd be doing that day and night for years."

"I didn't explain that well. Ask Him to forgive you for all the lies. Then confess resentment and jealousy or whatever comes to mind. He's asking you to trust Him for forgiveness and let Him love you."

"That's it?"

Euodia yawned. "That's the easy part. Remembering to ask for guidance and then choosing to obey is the hard part." She covered her mouth as another yawn surfaced. "I'm so sorry. Can we talk again tomorrow?"

Syntyche leaned forward and hugged Malitta. "If you'd like to talk more, come see me tomorrow. The feast of new beginnings is at Ty's house after church. You are welcome at both."

CHAPTER TWENTY-FOUR

Euodia slipped her arm through Syntyche's as they walked to church. She'd expected to be anxious, but soft peace filled her. Whether she and Syntyche were welcomed or shunned, forgiven or shamed, this standing before the other believers and asking for forgiveness was the right thing to do.

The courtyard was empty when they arrived. Side by side, they entered the building. Immediately, Syzygus called them forward amid murmurings and whispers. Hands clasped, they stood at the front. Euodia nodded in agreement as Syntyche spoke of their remorse and asked for forgiveness.

Silence followed. Silence so deep her ears rang. Euodia felt herself begin to sway and held Syntyche's hand tighter, grateful when Syntyche slipped an arm around her waist.

A woman Euodia did not recognize began to cry. "Forgive me, Syntyche. Your commitment to speaking truth shamed me, and I spread lies about you."

A mater and daughter stood. "Forgive us, Euodia."

Shock widened her eyes. Forgive *them*? Beside her, Syntyche had stiffened as if she too was unable to believe what she heard.

"We assumed the rumors and gossip were true but never sought the truth. We believed the worst of you."

"Syntyche, I've put you on a pedestal instead of seeing you as a woman who needs encouragement and friendship."

"We've let you carry our part of the responsibility."

"Sister, I never thanked you for helping me, but I've been quick to complain about you."

"Forgive me for turning away when you needed a friend."

"Sister Syntyche, I have smiled to your face and criticized you when your back was turned. Will you forgive me?"

Euodia wept as pleas for forgiveness poured forth from person after person.

At last, the confessions tapered off. Syzygus stepped forward and stood by the women. His red-rimmed eyes glowed.

"The Lord has blessed us with a time of reconciliation and healing. Let us give Him all praise and glory for His forgiveness and restoration. As we leave this place that is holy because of His presence, rejoice in His mercy and grace. Go in peace."

He touched Syntyche's shoulder. "These two women have prepared our second feast that will be held at their brother's home. Come, celebrate with us."

Something prickled Syntyche's neck. She brushed at the gnat or fly and continued to serve. It tickled again. A loose hair? She curved a finger around the back of her neck. No. It was almost as if she was being watched. Glancing over her shoulder, she saw nothing. Uneasy, she spun around when the prickling continued.

She searched the crowd. Clement had not attended, and Malitta was not here, but most of the other believers had arrived. They stood in small groups, eating, laughing, hugging one another. She searched again. Who was staring at her?

Ty's gaze met hers. Others might say he appeared nonchalant. She saw fury raging behind his still features.

Dry-mouthed, she elbowed Euodia and tilted her head toward their brother. Euodia too would realize Ty's displeasure. If she pinched the bridge of her nose the way Ty did, would it help her think?

Her mind raced for words. He'd specifically stated no Jews, no Christians, and no gatherings at his house, and he'd returned home to find it full of both groups. If he demanded they all leave, she could not fault him. Sighing, she imagined once again standing before the congregation and apologizing for the failed celebration.

Euodia grabbed her hand and began winding through the crowded room to where Ty stood waiting. With only a few steps to go, Brother Aaron barged in front and clapped a hand on Ty's shoulder.

"Greetings! Are you a new member or a guest? Either way, it matters not at all to me. I'm delighted to see you and welcome you to this lovely home. Oh, it's not mine, no indeed. The owner has most graciously and generously allowed us to use it just this once. I've never met him, but he must be kindness itself. Someday, I'll thank him on behalf of all of us."

Ty stared at the little man beaming up at him.

"Have you eaten? The food, no, the feast was prepared by these two magnificent women, these sisters. I must say, the food rivals that of my beloved mater's, God rest her soul, and that is not an easy feat. Come along, I will show you what to eat with what and which dishes to scoop extra onto your plate."

Aaron tucked his arm through Ty's and barreled forward. As he led him away, he twisted enough to wink at Euodia and Syntyche.

Euodia grinned. "I think Aaron knows that's our brother."

"And that he was not expecting nor pleased to find us gathered here." Syntyche tugged Euodia's hand. "Come on. I want to hear what else he says."

Trying to stay out of Ty's sight, they followed the two men as closely as possible.

Brother Aaron pointed to the challah. "See how it is braided? I've no idea if it's true, but my mater said it is because our lives are entwined like that. Our feast celebrates new beginnings, a time when wrongs have been righted because since we are entwined, what hurts you hurts me. Isn't that profound? Of course it is. My mater had great wisdom." He tore off a mound of the braided bread and held it out to Ty.

"Taste and tell me if it is not heaven itself. Yes?" Aaron chuckled. "Never knew heaven could be so delicious, did you? Go on, eat, eat. No need to be shy around this group."

Ty bit into the light, airy bread.

"It's a Jewish bread."

Ty choked.

"Jewish like me. These people are Greek, Jew, and Roman, slaves, servants, and masters. All believers in the Lord Jesus Christ. Do you know Him?"

"No."

Aaron clapped his hands. "Excellent. You have come to the right place to hear all about Him, but first, dip the challah in the hummus. It is perfection."

"I know. My sister—"

Aaron scurried away and returned with a dish of couscous. "Seven vegetables in this. Seven is a very important number to my people. Seven days of creation, on the seventh day we rest, and the first verse of Torah has seven words." He pushed the bowl into Ty's free hand. "Seven vegetables. Jewish food is very good."

Ty narrowed his eyes. "This is a Jewish feast?"

Aaron shrugged. "Perhaps. It's complicated. What does it matter? Good food does not need a reason to be savored, nor does the food care what race you claim. It is for everyone to enjoy." He rubbed his belly. "I like food. So do they, so do you. Look around. The people are happy. Smiling. Enjoying each other. In this world of so much tragedy, would you deny them a few moments of respite? They are at peace with themselves, their God, and each other. Are you?"

"Who are you?"

"Brother Aaron. Forgive me, Did I not say? Here, try the chicken with pomegranates—a little spicy, a little sweet, and beautiful, isn't it?

"Aaron, this is my house—"

Aaron threw wide his arms. "Yours? *You* are the gracious, generous owner? How can we ever thank you for your great kindness?"

He clapped his hands to gather attention, his voice booming over the scrape of utensils and chatter of the guests. "Friends, this is the man, our benefactor, the one who is so charitable in allowing us to meet here in his lovely home. Come, greet him with warmth and thanksgiving."

Ty stood, both hands full of food, as person after person came forward to thank him for agreeing to host them.

Euodia nudged her sister. "Synee, when everyone is gone, what will we do?"

Her heart warmed. "We will face him, together."

Brother Aaron was the last to leave the feast. In a sack, he carried a loaf of challah and a small bowl of hummus along with slices of meat.

"I will feast again tomorrow."

He peered at the empty room. Seeing no one to overhear him, he spoke solemnly. "You took a great risk for us. I pray your brother will forgive you."

Snatching a handful of dates, he bowed his head and left.

"Synee, where do you suppose he puts all that food he eats?"

"You were too young—just a baby—to remember Ty as a youth, but that's how he was, a nonstop eater. We couldn't keep food in the house."

"But Aaron is not a youth. He's old." Euodia lowered herself to a chair and pressed a hand against her back. "Ty will demand an explanation from us soon. Are you ready?"

"Should we go to him and not wait to be summoned like naughty children?"

"Let me sit and rest for another moment."

"Euodia, are you well?"

Euodia moistened her lips. "I've been hesitant to tell you and awaken your grief, but I'm—"

"With child! I should have known. Dearest, I'm so happy for you. You will be a wonderful mater, and I'll help in any way I can. What did Marcellus say when you told him?"

"I haven't told him."

"Told me what?" Marcellus entered the room. "Euodia, I see I'm too late for the feast, but I came despite my misgivings."

She slipped off the chair and wrapped her arms around him. "You tried. Thank you."

"I'd have made it back from the port in time except for the strangest thing. A man I knew years ago—we were not close friends, merely acquaintances—had arrived from Rome and stopped to feed his horse and eat at the same place I did." His stomach growled. "Is there any food left? It's been several hours and mishaps since I've eaten."

Syntyche handed him the last chunk of challah as Euodia piled leftovers on another plate.

"He overheard me mention Philippi and asked to ride here with me. Said he'd come to visit old friends and mentioned your brother. I offered to show him where Ty lives—I was coming here anyway—but he refused. Said he'd decided to make another stop first." Marcellus raised his hands in disbelief. "Then my horse lost a shoe, and I walked him home before coming here. Unbelievable, I know, but that's the reason I'm late."

"Marcellus, why did you come through the back entrance?" Euodia watched his face carefully. "Did you not want to be seen?"

"No one answered the front door. I heard voices—loud ones. The person your brother is speaking with has displeased him."

The confusion on Syntyche's face must have mirrored her own.

"He's upset with Synee and me for hosting the feast."

"And maybe the steward for allowing it?" He shrugged.

Euodia handed him the plate of food. "What changed your mind about coming here?"

He poked at the food so long, Euodia thought he'd not answer. "I realized there's a difference between believing in the Christ and living for the Christ."

Euodia pushed aside the plate and went into his arms.

"Sister."

They turned. Ty stood outside the open kitchen door, Marcus and Malitta behind him.

"Your God changes people. I see it in you." He turned to include Marcus and Malitta. "All of you. There's a difference, a newness. You live…forgiven. This Jesus of yours…" He rubbed the back of his neck. "You live in a light I don't have. I don't know how to explain it, but there's a darkness in me, an unfathomable darkness."

He pinched the bridge of his nose. "Four such different people who worship the same God, yet you have become of one mind."

His voice softened, his words not a command but a plea. "Tell me."

Letter from
THE AUTHOR

Dear Reader,

Days of Awe was a joy to write.

Faithful prayer warriors covered it in prayer, and almost immediately, the Lord guided me to a story we all share. *All* is a presumptuous word, yet I believe in this case, it's accurate.

While the writing was joy, the subject matter stepped on my toes. Repeatedly.

The subject? Comparison.

Comparison begins almost innocuously. "She looked…" "I wouldn't dream of letting…" "If I had her life, I'd…"

Comparison happens in church, in friendships, within yourself, toward yourself. It easily slides into judgment and competition, which can degenerate into bitterness and resentment.

Here's the scary part. Ultimately, we are not competing with others but with ourselves, our insecurities, our longing to be of more value than another—and that's called pride.

Do your toes hurt too?

I encourage you to offer your pride and comparison to the Lord. Ask Him to increase your awareness of judging others and considering yourself better or worse than another.

As the Holy Spirit increased an awareness of judging, I realized my comparisons were based on a perceived understanding of someone else and my personal definition of perfection—not the Lord's. Ouch. Transformation needed. Teach me, Lord!

Gratefully His,
Texie Susan Gregory

A SCHOLAR'S VIEW OF PHILIPPI

Thousands of years ago, Greek culture and life swept across ancient society, spreading art, philosophy, sculpture, architecture, and literature. The Greek perspective permeated the known world. Even after the Romans conquered the Greeks, the Greek ideals were not erased. Because the Romans respected Greek accomplishments, the world soon became a mix of both cultures. Such was true of ancient Philippi.

Located in what had been ancient Greece, Philippi bordered Rome's eastern province of Macedonia. The fertile plain surrounding the city's location had strategic value in that it connected the trade route linking the Aegean and Adriatic seas. Called the Egnatian Way, the ancient highway eventually led to Rome. Consequently, hotel businesses flourished in Philippi. Travelers walked through the city night and day, seeking shelter.

Several decades ago, I traveled across the area and stopped in Philippi. Archaeologists have uncovered much of the city, with the main street still running through the center. Greek influence produced a forum, a gymnasium, baths, a library, and an acropolis. Speculation suggests that large temples to the Greek gods Apollo and Artemis once existed there.

Philip II founded the original city in 360 BC, and then the Romans took over in 42 BC and reduced the size of the city.

However, Philippi remained Greek with a strong Roman influence. Many of the citizens were descendants of the original Greek settlers, and Philippi continued to be one of the most important cities in the region.

Veterans of Marc Antony's 23rd Legion, which defeated Cassius and Brutus, retired there. Antony's praetorian guards lost their claim to land in Italy, and over a thousand settled in the city. These veterans held agricultural estates worked by slaves. Because Philippi was a colony, it was considered an extension of Rome, granting the citizens Roman citizenship. This enabled self-government and tax exemption. By the time Paul arrived, there were around ten thousand enslaved persons who made up twenty percent of the population. Like all Roman cities, religious life provided a myriad of possibilities. With a large number of statues dedicated to her, the hunting goddess Diana—or Artemis to the Greeks—was probably the most popular.

Accompanied by Silas, Timothy, and Luke, Paul traveled to Philippi. While Paul normally went first to a synagogue to begin evangelizing, none existed in the city. So one Sabbath, Paul walked down to the riverbank to preach. One of the listeners was a Gentile named Lydia, who was to become his first convert in Europe. A merchant of purple cloth, Lydia had a sense of the one true God. As she listened to Paul, Lydia was drawn to his message and responded. The church in Philippi was born with important events to follow.

One of the most intriguing incidences occurred in Philippi's marketplace. An enslaved girl had a "spirit of divination." She disrupted worship by crying out during prayer. The possessed girl obviously created chaos.

The original Greek for "a spirit of divination" literally means "a spirit of Python," a serpent thought to live where the Oracle of Delphi existed in southern Greece. The Philippians probably thought that was what possessed the girl. The girl's owners used her for commercial purposes and profited from her illness, which was in and of itself a malicious act.

Paul's correction of the enslaved girl and expulsion of the demon resulted in the public officials being called, landing Paul and Silas in jail. When I visited Philippi, I went to what archaeologists believe to be the remnant of the jail. It is located up a hill overlooking the entire town.

One glance is enough to tell you what Roman prisons were like—dark and filthy, with people crowded together underground. They would have stunk. With inner and outer chambers, the innermost sections always stayed dreary. The inmates were chained together, so there was no escaping the squalor.

The Romans knew how to torture a confession out of their captives, physically and psychologically. Prisoners were often beaten into submission, and all dignity was stripped away. The darkness, filth, and inhumane conditions of imprisonment would tear a confession from even the innocent. Food was not provided for the prisoners. Their families were expected to bring sustenance. If they didn't, the incarcerated simply starved.

Though people might spend a great deal of time in a cell, there was no law that granted them time served in prison. Generally, prisoners were held until they were condemned to death. While there was a *Carcer Privatus*, a private prison, only debtors were kept there. The rest suffered in the *Custodia Privatus*, the public prison, with the full consequences of imprisonment and nothing but death before them. The entire system was meant to be a deterrent.

The Philippian church continued to be an important part of Paul's ministry before and after his release. On his third missionary journey, he returned. The congregation had given generous offerings to support his work. Even when Paul was imprisoned in Rome, he sent Epaphroditus to work with the Philippians. He also sent Timothy to this church, which became a strong and healthy congregation. As the apostolic age ended, the early church fathers continued their interest. Ignatius sojourned there, and Polycarp wrote what was to become his famous letter to the Philippians.

Today this ancient city lies in ruins on the fertile plains surrounding it. As one walks down the excavated streets where chariots once clattered, a few columns still reach into the sky. Every day of the week, people open their Bibles to read Paul's advice to the Philippians—and to us. Two thousand years later, we are still encouraged by Paul's words, "God will supply every need of yours according to his riches in glory in Christ Jesus."

Fiction Author

TEXIE SUSAN GREGORY

Every night when Texie Susan was a little girl, her mother, with an expressive voice and face, brought life to a Bible story. The stories became so familiar that sometimes the people seemed like distant relatives—Grandfather Abraham, Uncle Paul, Cousin Esther.

After discovering Elizabeth Speare's book *The Bronze Bow*, she realized people other than those she "knew" had lived and loved and laughed during Bible times. Astonishing!

Thus began her quest to write the stories of both the unknown and well-known people of biblical times.

Studying why people act and respond the way they do fascinates her. She has a master's degree in school counseling as well as in religious education.

North Carolina born and bred, Texie Susan and her husband are empty nesters living in Michigan, next door to their grandchildren.

Nonfiction Author
ROBERT L. WISE, Ph.D.

The Rev. Robert L. Wise, Ph.D., is the author of thirty-five books and numerous articles published in English, Spanish, Dutch, Chinese, Japanese, and German. On the internet he weekly publishes *Miracles Never Cease* and monthly presents live interviews on YouTube with people who have experienced divine interventions.

Read on for a sneak peek of another exciting story in the Extraordinary Women of the Bible series!

BELOVED BRIDE: RACHEL'S STORY

BY GINGER GARRETT

Glancing up, Rachel checked the sun's position. It was nearly noon. Time to lead the flock to the well. She'd give them a long, cool drink, followed by one last relaxed afternoon of grazing before leading them home. Leah would likely be done serving dinner and Father would be drinking with the men of the village.

Leah would sneak stew to her. She was a good sister who doted on Rachel as though she was her own lamb. The name *Rachel* meant "ewe" in Hebrew, so it was fitting. It was a mystery, really, why her father chose Hebrew names for the girls. They did not live among Hebrew people or in Hebrew lands. Aunt Rebekah had left years ago to marry a prince of Abraham, however. Maybe her father had hoped that a Hebrew prince would come for his daughters someday.

The thought made her laugh. The sheep bleated in response, slowly walking toward her as she moved down the path to the well. How many times had she followed the exact path through the spring grass and low shrubs? Maybe hundreds by now.

She'd been a shepherdess for two years, since her mother's death. Later this year, she'd finally be allowed to go into the mountains with the flock when the weather grew too hot here in the valley.

The path looked worn, her footsteps and her flock trampling the dirt into a flat, wide passageway she knew by heart. The sheep did too. She could lead them along it blindfolded. Sometimes that seemed like a marvelous ability. Today it depressed her. How badly she had once craved this job, this independence, this freedom from the stifling grief of home. Now she knew the grief could find her in the hills too, and life was no better. Different, but no better. This past winter had been bitter. The sting of grief still burned through the long, cloudless nights, a wound that had no remedy. The family's downfall had begun two summers ago, when Mother grew thin and began gasping for air at strange moments. Then the traders spread rumors of her sickness, and everyone avoided the area. Father's finances dwindled steadily as Mother's health deteriorated. When she finally died, her skin was so thin Rachel had been able to trace all the blue veins that ran beneath. The Egyptians had a name for it. They called it the Emperor of All Maladies, and it caused tumors that multiplied, causing great pain and weakness.

No one else contracted the disease, even though rumors warned it could be spread by bad air. It did not even seem to be a physical illness, but something from the dark underworld, a malevolent force, maybe the oldest curse and most powerful one. It was as if Death itself had awakened in her body, and, hour by hour, claimed everything it touched.

Rachel guessed the Egyptians, who had named it so well, might also know how to cure it, but their land was so far away to the South, past the Euphrates, past the mighty Nile. Father said the Egyptians had many books on sickness and medicine, but no healer from there had ever visited this region of Haran. Still, he kept one of their gods, Amun, on the household altar. If an Egyptian ever came through the area, Father would be ready.

Father had everyone's idols. That's why every trader, slaver, and merchant made his house a stop in their journeys. When traveling merchants came through Haran, they were delighted to break bread with Father, a man who supposedly worshiped their gods and obviously shared their understanding of the world.

Father was a shrewd man when he was sober. But he hadn't been sober since Mother died.

Rachel had never seen an Egyptian, but she hoped to. She would ask if the Emperor of All Maladies had ever been defeated. Great houses rose, great houses fell. What was the secret to bring this one down? Had any man found the answer?

She'd seen the traveling seers staring into bowls of herbs looking for signs. All she had to stare at was her flock. She'd never received any sign from them, of course. They were not ones to regard the heavens and ponder a mystery. A sheep never aspired to be anything but a sheep. They did not strive. That is what made them peaceful creatures to spend her days with. Besides that, they had such beautiful eyes.

There was no one she could unburden her heart to, except perhaps Shimean, an elderly shepherd she saw at the well.

Rachel had wanted to escape her grief. Father wanted to… what? Would Shimean understand and explain it? Father's grief had turned to greed. Father had always been a dreamer, but now he drank and slept during the best hours of the day.

Mother would be furious that he was allowing the girls to assume this much responsibility. Leah already cooked for the entire camp. The twins, Deen and Guri, were only seven and did not even have a tutor. They roamed the countryside like feral animals. Leah did her best to discipline them, but they only resented her for it.

Rachel understood Leah's attempts at discipline. Bandits and slavers roamed this wild country to the north of the Euphrates. Rachel could protect her flock from danger by using her wits but not her strength. Neither would protect her against armed men. She wished Father would give her a good dagger or buy a guard dog. But Father assigned her the job and did not want to hear of her difficulties.

The spring breeze was light, and the sun a delicate warmth across Rachel's face as she led her flock. She paused, lifting her face to the sun, wishing she could scoop up the day and put it in her pouch to carry home. It was simply that perfect, a day made for dancing after supper and chores and stargazing after Leah had extinguished the household lamp. Father had finished building their mud-brick home only three years ago, and the girls hated sleeping underneath a roof on nights like this.

With a grunt of dismay, Rachel saw a thorny vine entangled in a sheep's back flank as it passed. She pulled her little knife from her belt and approached the sheep gently. Distracted by the pleasant grasses, the sheep did not mind. Carefully, Rachel slit the wool free around the vine, but the vine remained tangled. She finally had to take the coat down to the skin and remove the vine still entangled in the wool. That's when she noticed that the wool on the underbelly was entangled too, and the vine had little tendrils that had worked into the flank on the other side. The sheep looked as if it had rolled in brambles and thorns. How could she have let this happen? This sheep had such a gorgeous coat!

That thought struck her in the heart like the blade of her knife. Father only raised the sheep to sell the fleece every spring. This sheep had a ruined fleece and would earn him nothing.

The animal wouldn't be able to grow its coat out in time for the shearing. If the wool was no good, Father would insist they get a return on the investment another way.

Fear shot through her knees. Would Father insist they butcher it for meat? She couldn't hide the large blank area over its back, and anyway, she wasn't the type of girl who deceived her father. He trusted her. That's why she was allowed to roam with the flock for days on end, without his supervision. She knew was trapped, her stomach twisting. Her little ewe was doomed.

Father could be unreasonable. If he was drunk, he could be cruel.

She kicked at a stone with the toe of her sandal. If Mother were here, she'd reason with Father and soften his temper.

Clicking her teeth, Rachel called for the flock, urging them toward the family well. At least her ewe could get that long, cool drink of water. The warm honey-gold eyes of the ewes mesmerized her. She adored the white fringe lashes on their lovely eyes, blinking lazily at her.

Straightening her back, Rachel scolded herself to think. She would see the other shepherds in the area, and they might have advice. They knew her father well. Everyone knew everything about everyone. That was life in Haran. There were no secrets.

A short walk later, she arrived at the well with her little flock. Three other area shepherds were already there, and she breathed a sigh of relief at their familiar faces. Though she would never admit this to Father, sometimes she was scared on her own.

The men waved cheerfully as she approached. It was custom to water the sheep only once the shepherds had all gathered. The land was owned by no one, but everyone depended on the well. This custom ensured that no one could ever be accused of taking more than a fair share. After all, if a well ran dry, it would mean disaster for the families and their flocks. All would have to move, or else dig and dig, hoping to find another source.

Shimean, the oldest and most patient of the shepherds, and her favorite, walked forward to greet her. Rachel was always allowed to water her little flock first. Maybe they felt sorry for her, a motherless girl with a big job. Or maybe they felt sorry for her father, having such a small flock and no one but her to care for them. Her two brothers were far too young to be shepherds.

Rachel didn't care what anyone thought. She was good at her job, and though her flock was small, she made sure they received the best care of any flock in the area.

Which is why she rested a hand on Shimean's arm a moment later, noticing the cracks in his skin, worn by the sun like old leather. She pressed her lips together, hard, warning her emotions to keep in check. Shimean was old, but that did not mean he was going to die. Mother's death had left her with a fear of everyone being ripped from her life without warning.

"What is it, my child?" he asked. He was the only adult who could call her that and still make it sound like a sign of respect.

Rachel explained her problem with the sheep and its ruined wool. "If Father realizes he won't get a fleece from it this year, he will butcher it."

The flocks bleated loudly, thirsty.

Shimean picked a piece of dry grass from her hair, flinging it away. "You are fond of this sheep?"

That would be a mistake, she knew. Shepherds treated their flocks as investments, not playthings.

Her chin dipped down before she could stop it, and hot tears filled her eyes. Grief swelled up at the worst moments, like a houseguest that would not leave. When would she ever be free of it? Not trusting herself to speak, she just nodded. She couldn't bear to see one butchered, especially not for her mistake. And letting the sheep wander into a tangled vine was certainly a mistake.

Shimean rested a hand on her head. She felt the weight of his big palm, the size of a fern leaf, as it covered her head, and the warmth seemed to soothe all her worries, as if it drew the dark thoughts from her mind.

She risked a glance and looked up at him. His lips were a thin line, and one eyebrow arched as he studied her face.

"I think...," he murmured then glanced at his own flock. "I think your sheep is exactly the same color as mine. See?"

She followed his gaze. He was crazy. His sheep were gorgeous. Their coats were purest white. He sold every fleece for the highest price in the region.

"Take my sheep," Shimean said, "and I will take yours. An even trade."

"But the wool is ruined!" Rachel said. "And I like her." She added that part softly, embarrassed.

Shimean laughed, but in a way that made Rachel want to laugh too.

"After shearing season, we'll trade back," Shimean said with a wink. "No one will be any wiser."

Rachel bit her lip, considering the offer. She did not want to trick her father. But what if that was the only way to save the sheep? Was it justified to trick Father if the outcome was good? He would be thrilled with the price the fleece brought.

Her shoulders slumped. "I can't." She smiled at Shimean. "Thank you. You are wise and kind. But I cannot trick him. It would weigh on my conscience."

Shimean shrugged lightly. "I understand. But take comfort in this—your father is shrewd. He won't butcher her if you can convince him that next year's fleece will be worth a great deal."

"How can you be so sure?" Rachel asked, feeling as if she were putting her foot into a fast-moving stream. This could go badly, but she didn't know quite yet, not until she had her full weight committed.

A shepherd called out, and Shimean lifted a hand to signal they were almost done.

"Your father has eyes like a serpent. I mean no disrespect," Shimean added quickly. "But have you ever noticed the way he watches, unblinking, as the traders ply their wares at the market?"

"He looks so bored."

"Not bored. Listening." Shimean wagged a finger at her. "Don't you know that's why he gets the best prices? He knows when the vendors are tired or discouraged. He listens to gossip and knows who is desperate."

Rachel looked up, trying to recall Father's expression. The market was hosted at her family compound once a week, because her father had an altar and stone gods. He was the only man in the area with so many stone idols, each from different lands. The nomads and traders liked to stop and worship, pleasantly surprised to see their god worshiped far from home. Laban's home became a central stopping point and then a meeting point, and when he had suggested creating a weekly market at his home, many families were pleased.

Rachel had considered this all to be good fortune, brought about by the gods her father worshiped. She had never once considered that a man might arrange his own fortunes.

Her knees felt unsteady as if the river's floor shifted, just slightly. Shrewd, indeed.

"Your father will force himself to wait another year to get what he wants, whether that's wool or meat," Shimean said, a final note in his voice. He had convinced himself, at least, but Rachel was the one with a life at risk. The uncertainty made her queasy. She studied Shimean's worn, lined face. He'd seen much in his many years. Could his advice be trusted?

He had never failed her in the past. She chewed her lip. Were there any other options? None she could think of.

A wind stirred from the west, from the sea, driving dull heavy clouds over the flocks.

"Open the well," Shimean called. As the oldest shepherd, he alone had the right to order the stone be removed.

The men immediately knelt together to push the stone aside and began watering the flocks. All the sheep rushed to the long trough and dipped their heads.

"We should move the flocks to their shelters for the night," Shimean said, not waiting for her to decide. He walked back toward his flock. "I think it may rain. Pity. No chance for a last graze for them."

Rachel nodded and thanked him. She had relied on him and the other shepherds so many times since her mother's death, and since her father had shut down and shut himself away in his mind. But trusting Shimean had been a leap of faith, and it had always paid off.

After the watering, she urged the sheep toward home. They trotted happily along because they trusted her. She couldn't risk getting caught in a storm with them.

As she followed, she glanced back toward the west, where travelers said a vast sea was. She'd never seen it. She'd never seen anything, nor had she wanted to. Still, the winds came, bringing storms.

How was it possible that a place she had never seen could impact her life?

A Note from
THE EDITORS

We hope you enjoyed another exciting volume in the Extraordinary Women of the Bible series, published by Guideposts. For over seventy-five years, Guideposts, a nonprofit organization, has been driven by a vision of a world filled with hope. We aspire to be the voice of a trusted friend, a friend who makes you feel more hopeful and connected.

By making a purchase from Guideposts, you join our community in touching millions of lives, inspiring them to believe that all things are possible through faith, hope, and prayer. Your continued support allows us to provide uplifting resources to those in need. Whether through our communities, websites, apps, or publications, we inspire our audiences, bring them together, and comfort, uplift, entertain, and guide them. Visit us at guideposts.org to learn more.

We would love to hear from you. Write us at Guideposts, P.O. Box 5815, Harlan, Iowa 51593 or call us at (800) 932-2145. Did you love *Days of Awe: Euodia and Syntyche's Story*? Leave a review for this product on guideposts.org/shop. Your feedback helps others in our community find relevant products.

While you are waiting for the next fascinating story in the Extraordinary Women of the Bible series, check out our other Guideposts biblical fiction series!

ORDINARY WOMEN OF THE BIBLE

From generation to generation and every walk of life, God seeks out women to do His will. Scripture offers us but fleeting, tantalizing glimpses into the lives of a number of everyday women in Bible times—many of whom are not even named in its pages. In each volume of Guideposts' Ordinary Women of the Bible series, you'll meet one of these unsung, ordinary women face to face, and see how God used her to change the course of history.

A Mother's Sacrifice: Jochebed's Story

The Healer's Touch: Tikva's Story

The Ark Builder's Wife: Zarah's Story

An Unlikely Witness: Joanna's Story

The Last Drop of Oil: Adaliah's Story

A Perilous Journey: Phoebe's Story

Pursued by a King: Abigail's Story

An Eternal Love: Tabitha's Story

Rich Beyond Measure: Zlata's Story

The Life Giver: Shiphra's Story

No Stone Cast: Eliyanah's Story

Her Source of Strength: Raya's Story

Missionary of Hope: Priscilla's Story

Befitting Royalty: Lydia's Story

The Prophet's Songbird: Atarah's Story

Daughter of Light: Charilene's Story

The Reluctant Rival: Leah's Story

The Elder Sister: Miriam's Story

Where He Leads Me: Zipporah's Story

The Dream Weaver's Bride: Asenath's Story

Alone at the Well: Photine's Story

Raised for a Purpose: Talia's Story

Mother of Kings: Zemirah's Story

The Dearly Beloved: Apphia's Story